U0062863

IELTS
Listening

雅思听力
真题词汇精讲

宋鹏昊 齐小霞 编著

浙江教育出版社·杭州

雅思考试的设计非常科学，考生的考试体验也非常好，因此越来越多的考生将雅思考试成绩作为自己出国留学语言成绩的第一选择，同时也有越来越多的学生出于求职、能力提升、证明自身语言水平等目的，选择参加雅思考试，这也让雅思考试充分发挥其作为"一把衡量英语水平的统一标尺"的功能。

与中学和大学的英语考试不同，雅思考试的备考多是"个人行为"，多数考生需要独立制订学习规划并完成整个学习过程，因此除了英语学习本身之外，信息的检索和分析筛查能力、计划的制订和执行能力、承担压力与孤独的能力、考前心态的调整等都是获得优秀分数所必需的。在本书的序言部分，我会针对雅思备考的几个重要问题进行阐述，以期帮助考生对考试有正确的认知，而之后的每个章节则是非常具体的学习和练习内容，帮助考生在雅思听力方面打下坚实的基础。

雅思考试的核心是什么

雅思考试是一种高度标准化的语言能力测试，考查的是考生的语言能力，这就意味着考试的核心离不开"技能"、"熟练度"、"能力"这几个关键词，所以雅思考试不是一个针对知识的考试，比如中学阶段的历史考试，而更类似于考查一个人弹钢琴、画画、打篮球能力的考试，这些都是需要使用技能的，并且对考生的熟练度有一定要求。这就解释了为什么让很多考生感到头疼的是听力录音只放一遍，要在 60 分钟内完成 40 道阅读题目，文章长度还都很长，而写作则需要在 60 分钟内写出五六百个单词，这实际上都是对熟练度的考查，通过考查熟练度来考查能力。试想如果听力录音放两遍，阅读考试时间一个半小时，那么考试的难度一下子就降低了，也就无法很好地区分出不同考生运用英语的熟练程度了。

雅思备考的核心是什么

了解了雅思考试的核心，备考的核心问题也就迎刃而解了。对于任何技能，提升熟练度最简单的方法都是 Time on Task，也就是在这件事上花的时间和重复的遍数。举一个很简单的例子：把一首曲子弹奏 200 遍的人和弹奏 20 遍的人，他们再次弹奏作品时，我们大都可以快速分辨出高下。同样，画过 500 个小时画的人和画过 50 个小时画的人，我们也可以很快区分出他们的作品。对于几乎任何技能而言，上面的例子都适用。

因此，对于雅思学习和备考，听更多音频，读更多文章，写更多作文，口头回答更多问题，就是考试之前要做的最重要的事情。而掌握本书中的听力考点词汇，恰恰是在听力这个科目上要做的第一件事。所以，把这本书用好，学会书中所有的词汇，并反复练习，会让考生之后的备考之旅顺畅很多。

听力备考的常见误区

在听力的备考中，很多考生存在如下几个学习误区，这导致了效率的低下。

第一个误区是很多考生不对听力词汇进行系统学习。不少考生急于尝试做真题，跳过了夯实基础的阶段，但做题时无法完全听懂听力原文，无法准确找到题目对应的音频中的内容，填空时也经常出现拼写问题，究其原因是考生没有系统学习过听力词汇，这时就重复刷题实际上没有太大的效果。

第二个常见误区是把听力当成阅读去学习，过于关注文本信息而忽略听觉信息。雅思听力的输入信息都是以音频形式出现的，且只出现一次，试卷上的文本所包含的重要信息其实并不多。因此备考中更应该关注的是能不能用耳朵听懂听觉信息，以及能否把要填写的单词准确地拼写出来。在使用本书时，也请重视音频的使用，重视听写的准确性。

最后一个常见误区是不少考生存在"学习知识"的误区，认为自己好像学会了，就把复习材料放一边，却忽略了任何技能都会"用进废退"，练习一停就会"手生"这一原则。这种情况在听力考试中尤其适用。当考生看到听力中常考的单词时，很多时候不会认为它们有多大难度，反而会觉得这些词都非常熟悉。但要切记，雅思听力考试考查的是熟练度，而且是听觉的熟练度，这就意味着实际考试中没有多少反应时间，也看不到音频的文本，并且也没有多少蒙混过关的机会，每写错一个数字或一个字母都可能影响最终的分数，所以考前保持规律的练习至关重要。除了在学习的最初阶段使用本书，对本书的学习还可以贯穿整个备考过程，并且要确保考前熟练掌握书中的每一个单词。

学习中必备的几种能力

如前文所言，雅思考试除了考查考生的英语能力外，也考查考生的综合能力。考生要想获得不错的分数，至少要具备以下三种能力。

首先，考生需要具备合理规划学习和生活的能力。无论中学生、大学生，还是职场人士，都需要根据自己的时间合理规划学习和生活，这就意味着考生要清楚自己学习中可能出现的疲劳或懒惰，清楚自己越到考前越可能焦虑，清楚自己很难一整天保持精力高度集中的状态，基于自身的情况规划自己的学习和生活。顺利完成可行的规划比制订理想的规划更加重要。

其次，考生需要具备寻求帮助和支持的能力。无论是同学还是老师，大都能在不同方面帮助到你。过去十几年的时间里，无论作为老师还是学生，我也深切体会到学习中同伴和师长所起到的作用。无论他们能够给你讲课，教你做题，为你答疑，帮助你批改作文，帮助你进行口语模考，还是单纯地聊聊天，帮你放松心情、缓解压力，这些支持和帮助都会让你的备考之旅轻松许多。你也可以通过我的微信公众号（ID: songpenghao666）与我进行交流，寻求帮助。

另外，考生还需具备持之以恒的能力。实际上，雅思考试并不是一个难度巨大的考试，保质保量地完成复习中应该做的事情，获得一个不错的分数是水到渠成的。如果能在备考雅思的过程中让自己养成优秀的学习习惯，能够保持专注，持之以恒地做完该做的事情，那么这无疑对未来的生活和事业都会有莫大帮助。

最后，感谢各位考生选择使用这本书进行备考，希望大家能够按照科学合理的计划，认真学习完本书内容，并在备考中经常拿出来练习，以提高熟练度，在考试中有好的表现。祝每位考生都可以有一段愉快又充满收获的雅思备考之旅，早日获得一个让自己足够欣喜的分数！

编者　宋鹏昊

在雅思备考中，多数考生会像准备其他考试一样，兵马未动，粮草先行，而词汇就是打赢雅思考试这场硬仗的"粮草"。

雅思词汇大致可以分为两类。一类是不按照考试科目区分的通用词汇，很多考生使用这类词汇书，书中的单词有些按首字母顺序排列，有些按词汇在考试中出现的频率排列，有些按照词汇的难度排列，还有一些乱序排列。学习这类词汇能夯实词汇基础，每天大量背诵并做好巩固复习，熟悉词义，快速识别。词汇量大的考生在阅读中能展现出巨大优势，阅读速度会更快，也能更准确地理解句子。另一类词汇是以雅思听、说、读、写四个科目进行划分的专项词汇，例如这本《雅思听力真题词汇精讲》，就是专门针对雅思听力真题考点编写的。听力考试对考生掌握单词的准确性要求较高，要求考生能够快速听音识词，并且拼写正确，因此本书中对不同考点词的拼写规则进行总结，并配备习题供考生反复练习。雅思听力考试涉及生活类和学术类场景，听力原文和题目、答案之间会有同义替换，与之相应，本书包含对听力场景词和同义替换词的总结。把对通用词汇的学习和针对不同科目的词汇的学习相结合，会起到强化学习效果的作用。

具体到本书的内容，经过反复推敲与研讨，最终呈献在考生手中的这本听力词汇以雅思历年考试真题和"剑桥雅思真题集"为依托，共分为三个章节：

第一章讲解雅思听力真题考点词。本章重点打牢考生的词汇基本功，针对雅思听力填空题中可能出现的数字、地址、日期、字母与数字、连字符、英美式拼写等考点进行专项训练，帮助考生了解单词和短语的发音及拼写规则。本章的第二节加入了多音词、同音异形词及发音相近词，配合音频做听写练习，有助于考生识别发音和形态易混淆的单词。第三节精选了近年雅思真题题干、选项及答案中提取出的高频考点词，并按照不同词性分类。对这些单词，在考试中不仅需要快速听音识别，还需要准确拼写。

第二章聚焦于雅思听力场景词汇的学习。雅思听力共有四个部分，其中 Part 1 和 Part 2 考查生活场景，Part 3 和 Part 4 考查学术场景。录音无论是独白还是对话，说话者都会围绕此话题进行陈述或讨论。不同场景涉及不同主题的词汇，第二章将同一场景中经常出现的单词称为"听力场景词"。熟悉场景词的考生可以在听到大段内容时快速沉浸在这一场景中，缩短对陌生词汇的反应时间，对答案词进行快速预判。本章包含住宿、饮食、旅游、健康等八大场景，覆盖了雅思听力全部常见主题。

第三章讲解雅思听力中重要的同义替换词。雅思考试的听、说、读、写四个部分对考生识别和运用同义替换词的能力都有考查，同义替换词体现了词汇的多样性，避免说话时的重复，是语言学习的重要内容。雅思听力考试并非简单的听写，考生在听到录音中的大段内容时，不仅要听懂大意，还要对听到的词句和看到的题干信息进行判断，填写或选择出符合要求的答案。对同义替换词不敏感的考生会错过答案词出现的位置，并因此错失答题良机。本章提取了剑桥雅思真题中听力原文和题干中的同义替换词，并仔细筛选，选出了400组最具代表性的词汇供考生学习。

听力词汇与阅读词汇相比，看似难度级别较低，但在真实考试中，考查的是考生在听到词汇的瞬间，快速识别其在句中的语义，并在听力过程中同时确认答案词并正确地拼写出来。所以在使用这本书时，考生一定要结合音频进行听写练习，不断加强听音辨音能力，争取在走上考场前将拼写正确率提高到100%。

除了应对试卷上的题目，备考雅思听力还会帮助考生了解和体会出国后会遇到的生活和学习情境，学会寻求帮助，理解他人的表达，与同学沟通学术难题，抓住教授讲座重点等。从这个意义上讲，备考中的每次练习也都是为出国之后更好地融入当地生活和学习做准备。希望每位考生能扎实练习，早日获得高分，实现自己的留学梦想！

编者　齐小霞

目录

01
CHAPTER

雅思听力真题
考点词

本章音频

词汇既是学好听力的基础，也是雅思听力的重要考点。本章精选了历年雅思真题中的真实考点，按照考试难度编排，分别针对基础考点、发音与拼写、高频考点词进行总结，分门别类地呈现真实雅思考试中的听力考点。

第一节　基础考点

一　纯数字

数字听写是雅思听力 Part 1 的高频考点，中文和英文在数字表达上的差异让许多考生对数字听写束手无策。要掌握数字听写的基本技巧，首先要学会数字的英语读法。英语中的数字是三位数一划分，以千（thousand）、百万（million）、十亿（billion）和万亿（trillion）为单位，例如剑 5–Test 3–Part 4 中的第 35 题出现的对数字的考查："In the UK, 500,000 (five hundred thousand) tons of glass is recycled each year."。另外，百位数和十位数之间需要加上 and，比如 218 读作 two hundred and eighteen。

真题中还多次出现了对"十几"和"几十"的辨音考查，例如：

剑 5–Test 1–Part 1 中的第 7 题：The tour costs $280 (two hundred and eighty).

剑 8–Test 2–Part 1 中的第 10 题：Okay, so that would be around $60 (sixty) altogether?

剑 11–Test 1–Part 1 中的第 2 题：So from six pm to midnight that'd be £115 (a hundred and fifteen).

剑 14–Test 1–Part 1 中的第 4 题：But there was quite a bit of cash there... about £250 (two hundred and fifty) sterling.

剑 14–Test 1–Part 1 中的第 4 题：But there was quite a bit of cash there... about £250 (two hundred and fifty) sterling.

剑 17–Test 1–Part 1 中的第 10 题：There's a charge of £35 (thirty-five), including lunch, or £40 (forty) if you want to camp in the wood.

真题考点示范

听录音，并朗读下列数字，保证熟悉每个数字的发音，并能够进行分辨。

学习后，可完成练习册中对应的练习，以提升听力能力。

14	19	26	50	66
80	100	318	390	558
581	619	818	889	918
980	1,000	1,115	1,490	1,700
2,280	2,800	3,182	4,518	5,580
6,600	8,412	9,920	10,000	55,000
12,520	22,100	78,000	100,000	131,000
260,819	385,900	661,922	1,000,000	236,400,000

二 长数字

长数字是雅思听力 Part 1 的考点之一，常见的考试形式包括银行卡号、电话号码和编号等。对考生来说，长数字的听写难度比较大，原因是数字比较长，而且只能听一遍。在录音中，长数字的朗读按照基本数字读法，说话人在朗读时会每三位或者四位稍作停顿。例如，剑 14–Test 1–Part 1 的第 10 题："So what I'm going to do now is give you a crime reference number so you can contact your insurance company. So this is ten digits: 87954 82361 (eight seven nine five four eight two three six one)."。剑 14–Test 2–Part 1 中的第 1 题也出现了对长数字的考查："And can I have a contact phone number? It's 219 442 9785 (two one nine four four two nine seven eight five)."。

在朗读时，出现连续两个相同的数字多读作"double + 数字"，连续三个相同的数字多读作"triple + 数字"，数字 0 常被读作"O [əʊ]"或者"zero"。例如剑 11–Test 2–Part 1 的第 10 题："Yes, my mobile number's 07788 136711 (O double seven double eight one three six seven double one)."。

真题考点示范

听录音，并朗读下列卡号、电话号码或编号，保证熟悉每串数字的发音，并能够进行分辨。

学习后，可完成练习册中对应的练习，以提升听力能力。

765009288	264796623	800045873	726940504	893007792
987023221	405067930	233888672	617289038	2225556729
6644882910	7783320001	576000121	23192813121	891007216
310987111	1229870061	7832223987	9872361	12978083
7826300421	90082741	8002831220	568219003	4574592831
98010231	501666832	3281919	0650920345	94419829
287644	8920047592			

三 字母与数字

雅思听力真题出现字母与数字组合多与编号有关，比如车牌号、课程编号、护照号、邮编等。编号中的数字按照基本数字读法，逐一朗读。数字 0 常被读作 "O [əʊ]" 或者 "zero"。字母 Z 可以被读作 "[zed]" 或者 "[ziː]"。编号中出现连续两个相同的数字，多读作 "double + 数字"；连续三个相同的数字，多读作 "triple + 数字"；同理，出现连续两个或者三个字母可以读作 "double + 字母" 或者 "triple + 字母"。此外，在答题时，建议将编号中的字母大写。

邮编也是字母和数字的组合，定义了地理单位的不同级别。雅思听力中通常逐位（digit by digit）朗读邮编，但是偶尔也有例外，部分地区的邮编由两部分组成，例如 SO15 2GB 是由外向编码 SO15 和内向编码 2GB 构成。这类邮编读作 "S-O-fifteen 2-G-B"。

具体情况可以参考以下真题示例：

剑 7–Test 4–Part 1 中的第 2 题：

Okay... your passport number is JO 6337 (J-O-six-double three-seven).

剑 8–Test 1–Part 1 中的第 4 题：

−Do you remember our new postcode?

−WS6 2YH (W-S-six two-Y-H).

剑 10–Test 2–Part 1 中的第 3 题：

−Is the post code GT7?

−It's actually GT8 2LC (G-T-eight two-L-C).

剑 12–Test 4–Part 1 中的第 8 题：

−And what's the postcode, please?

−DG7 4PH (D-G-seven four-P-H).

真题考点示范

听录音，并朗读下列字母与数字组合，保证熟悉它们的发音，并能够进行分辨。学习后，可完成练习册中对应的练习，以提升听力能力。

DJ745PQ	SCF008	ARBU808	457ELPS
ROLS915	DPS473	LOP342MHU	GRO2180
LYNE288HG	DUW05444	SCUU8934	LMNP098
DH55 4SW	E14 5HQ	CV35 0DB	CF99 1NA
G58 1SB	SO14 1OB	G88 SH2	JHD11 L90
AB14 526	338PAPA	GHMM420	KIKO230
FEN1287	COUR541	FORE5ST	THER808
YIHON8764	RETS628	POPA278	NIEC561RS
782BUTH	TREO5S1MN	RORS8VV0	LOPS187HN
99AAEOO			

四　单位

雅思听力关于单位的考查多与货币单位有关，其中英镑（pound，符号为 £）是重点考查的货币单位。读金额时，1 英镑读作 one pound，2 英镑读作 two pounds。遇到小数点时，pound 应在整数之后读，例如 £4.50 读作 four pounds fifty。Part 1 中涉及花费、薪酬时，需要考生准确写出金额。值得注意的是，在绝大多数情况下，考生只需要写数字，不需要写货币单位。此外，除了货币单位，真题题干中也会出现面积单位 hectare、体积单位 litre、重量单位 ton 等词汇。

具体情况可以参考以下真题示例：

剑 8-Test 1-Part 3 中的第 28 题：

—What area does the tribal park cover?

—12,000 (twelve thousand) hectares.

剑 9–Test 1–Part 1 中的第 4 题：

−And could I ask about the pay?

−We're offering £4.45 (four pounds forty-five) an hour.

剑 13–Test 3–Part 1 中的第 1 题：

You should be able to get something reasonable for £850 (eight hundred and fifty) per month.

剑 15–Test 4–Part 1 中的第 5 题：

−So you paid the full price for your ticket?

−I paid £23.70 (twenty-three pounds seventy).

听力中常见的单位

yuan 元	pound 英镑	dollar 美元	euro 欧元
yen 日元	degree Celsius 摄氏度	degree Fahrenheit 华氏度	inch 英寸
foot 英尺	yard 码	mile 英里	millimetre 毫米
centimetre 厘米	metre 米	kilometre 千米	square metre 平方米
cubic metre 立方米	litre 升	gallon 加仑	ounce 盎司
pint 品脱	gram 克	kilogram 千克	ton 吨
joule (J) 焦耳	kilowatt (kW) 千瓦	volt (V) 伏特	ampere 安培

真题考点示范

听录音，并朗读下列单位的表达，保证熟悉它们的发音，并能够进行分辨。

学习后，可完成练习册中对应的练习，以提升听力能力。

£7.45	£60.50	$14.80	120 hectares
80 square metres	1.4 litres	250 tons	1,300 cubic metres
500,200 kilometres	500 miles	10 centimetres	3–4 pints

| 80 grams | 200 gallons | 880 ounces | 1,000 amperes |
| 280 yards | 6 inches | 20 degrees Celsius | 90 degrees Fahrenheit |

五 地址

雅思听力考试中经常涉及关于地址的考点。英语中的地址表达往往按照从小到大的顺序排列：从 house number and street number 到 town，再到 city，之后是 state 和 country。其中对"门牌号＋街道名称＋道路"的考查最为频繁。

门牌号就是一般数字。街道名称有两种考法：一种是考查简单名词，大多是考查自然事物，比如 hill、bank、forest 等；另一种是考查拼写，录音中说话人会把街道名称拼读出来。考生在跟听拼写时，需要注意确保拼写正确，同时不要忘记写街道名称后面的 road 或 street。

具体情况可以参考以下真题示例：

剑 5–Test 4–Part 1 中的第 1 题：Sea View Guest House, 14 Hill Road.

剑 9–Test 1–Part 1 中的第 2 题：We have two branches–the one we're recruiting for is in Hillsdunne Road. It's H-I-double L-S-D-U-double N-E Road.

剑 10–Test 3–Part 1 中的第 2 题：It's 46 Wombat Road, that's W-O-M-B-A-T.

剑 11–Test 2–Part 1 中的第 2 题：That's 17, Buckleigh Street, B-U-C-K-L-E-I-G-H Street, Stamford Lincolnshire.

剑 17–Test 3–Part 1 中的第 4 题：There's a good surf school at Carrowniskey beach. C-A-double R-O-W-N-I-S-K-E-Y.

听力中常见的地址

| avenue 大道 | drive 车道 | road 道路 | street 街道 |
| lane 弄 / 巷 | square 广场 | circle 环路 | |

真题考点示范

听录音，并朗读下列地址的表达，保证熟悉它们的发音，并能够进行分辨。

学习后，可完成练习册对应章节的练习，以提升听力能力。

14 Bank Road	25 Bridge Road	Station Square	11 Arbuthnot Road
23 Riverside Street	7th Sunflower Avenue	Oxford Street	Regent Street
Abbey Road	Portobello Avenue	No. 4 Fleet Lane	11 King Street
13 Ocean Road	5th Avenue	Woodside Street	Crawley Street
No. 8 Chelsea Road	Mayfair Avenue	Anton Street	15 Islington Road
Fernlea Square	Balham Street	Battersea Road	58 Carter Lane
127 Dulwich Road	No.1 Canary Street	20 Great Sutton Street	25 Canonbury Lane
46 Smithfield Street	69 Camden Road	317 Finchley Road	

六 日期

雅思听力中日期书写为"月日年"或者"日月年"，月份与日期中间需要空一格，年份前需要加逗号","。需要注意月份要写成单词形式，不可以使用缩写，比如"Feb."。日期可以直接写成数字，无须再加序数词词尾变化（st/nd/rd/th），也无须将 st/nd/rd/th 写成角标。另外，还需要注意填空题的词数限制，如果词数限制为 NO MORE THAN ONE WORD OR A NUMBER，可以用"."或者"-"将数字连在一起，比如 23.10.1999。

具体情况可以参考下列真题：

剑 5–Test 1–Part 1 中的第 3 题：There's one in three weeks' time which is April the 18th.

剑 6–Test 3–Part 1 中的第 2 题：

—And what's your date of birth, please?

—The twenty-seventh of the first, nineteen seventy-three. (27.01.1973)

剑 8–Test 2–Part 1 中的第 3 题：

It left on the 11th of October and got to Sydney on the 28th of November.

剑 14–Test 2–Part 1 中的第 2 题：

—And then can I just check that we have the correct date of birth?

—October tenth, 1992.

剑 17–Test 3–Part 1 中的第 7 题：

September's my favourite month because the water is warmer then.

听力中常见的日期表达

Monday 星期一	Tuesday 星期二	Wednesday 星期三	Thursday 星期四
Friday 星期五	Saturday 星期六	Sunday 星期天	January 一月
February 二月	March 三月	April 四月	May 五月
June 六月	July 七月	August 八月	September 九月
October 十月	November 十一月	December 十二月	

真题考点示范

听录音，并朗读下列日期的表达，保证熟悉它们的发音，并能够进行分辨。

学习后，可完成练习册中对应的练习，以提升听力能力。

May 1	11 June	21 August	22 October
27 September	April 19, 1998	23 March, 2004	31 January, 1976
20 February, 2021	24 December, 1960	November 12, 2008	April 2
19 January, 1994	24 February, 2000	22 June, 1980	July 27
August 19	May 7, 1919	March 18, 2018	21 December
29 November, 1988	30 October	January 1, 2001	10 August, 1830
23 December, 2005	July 15	11 November	8 October, 1949
September 18, 2015	15 March	3 February	

七 时间

英语中的时间可以按照顺读法和倒读法来朗读，雅思听力主要考查顺读法。顺读法也叫直接读法，先读钟点数，再读分钟数。如果读的时间是整点数，则读作"钟点数 + o'clock"，o'clock 可以省略。如果要读的时间的分钟数是 30 分钟，读作"钟点数 + thirty"。

倒读法是与顺读法完全相反的读法，先读时间的分钟数，再读钟点数。需要注意以下三点：

- 如果分钟数少于 30 分钟，可用"分钟 + past + 钟点"表示，其中 past 是介词，意思是"过"。例如，twenty past four 表示 4 点 20 分，eight past one 表示 1 点 08 分。

- 如果分钟数多于 30 分钟，可用"（60 分钟 − 原分钟数）+ to + （原钟点数 + 1）"表示，其中 to 是介词，意思是"差"。例如，eighteen to three 表示 2 点 42 分，five to six 表示 5 点 55 分。

- 15 分钟可以用名词 quarter 表示，30 分钟可以用名词 half 表示。比如 a quarter to ten 表示 9 点 45 分，half past eleven 表示 11 点 30 分。

此外，时间的书写方式有两种，以 2 点 30 分为例，既可以写作 2.30，也可以写作 2:30。

具体情况可以参考以下真题示例：

剑 5−Test 4−Part 1 中的第 2 题：

I suppose between 9 and, let me see, half-past, (9:00−9:30) before I leave for the college.

剑 9−Test 1−Part 1 中的第 6 题：

If you're working after 11 o'clock (eleven o'clock) we drive you home.

剑 10−Test 3−Part 1 中的第 4 题：

I need to get to work in the city by 9:00 (nine) so I'll drop her off at 8:30 (eight thirty).

剑 11−Test 2−Part 1 中的第 9 题：

−Would you like to suggest a time?

−Would 4.30 (four thirty) be OK?

真题考点示范

听录音，并朗读下列时间的表达，保证熟悉它们的发音，并能够进行分辨。

学习后，可完成练习册中对应的练习，以提升听力能力。

10:00	10:15	8:30	9:25	7:20	5:40
6:45	4:58	5:05	10−10.30	8:00	9:45
6:30	10:25	7:10	11:05	11:35	7:37
9:15	8:50	2:20	3:15	6:18	10:55

第二节　发音与拼写

一　多音词

英语中一些单词既可以作名词，也可以作动词。一般作名词时重音在前，作动词时重音在后。考生需注意这两种词性要表达的意思也是相关联的，例如 survey 作名词时读作 ['sɜːveɪ]，意思是"调查、测量"；作动词时读作 [sə'veɪ]，意思是"调查，测量"。

一些单词作名词和动词时，重音位置不变，但是某些发音会改变。通常作名词时是清辅音，作动词时是浊辅音；或者作名词时是短元音，作动词时是长元音。例如，close 作名词时读作 [kləʊs]，意思是"死胡同"；作动词时读作 [kləʊz]，意思是"关闭"。

还有一些单词在不同领域或者表达不同含义时发音不同。例如，lead 作名词时读作 [led]，意思是"铅"；作动词时读作 [liːd]，意思是"领导"。

以下词汇需重点掌握

单词	音标及释义	单词	音标及释义
contract	['kɒntrækt] n. 合同 [kən'trækt] v.（使）收缩	conduct	['kɒndʌkt] n. 行为；举止 [kən'dʌkt] v. 组织；处理
digest	['daɪdʒest] n. 文摘 [daɪ'dʒest] v.（使）消化	extract	['ekstrækt] n. 提取物 [ɪk'strækt] v. 提取
escort	['eskɔːt] n. 护送者 [ɪ'skɔːt] v. 护送	impact	['ɪmpækt] n. 冲击 [ɪm'pækt] v. 对…产生影响
desert	['dezət] n. 沙漠 [dɪ'zɜːt] v. 抛弃	record	['rekɔːd] n. 记录 [rɪ'kɔːd] v. 记录，记载
insert	['ɪnsɜːt] n. 插入物 [ɪn'sɜːt] v. 插入	insult	['ɪnsʌlt] n. 辱骂 [ɪn'sʌlt] v. 侮辱
rebel	['rebl] n. 反抗者 [rɪ'bel] v. 反叛	present	['preznt] n. 礼物 [prɪ'zent] v. 呈现

单词	音标及释义	单词	音标及释义
project	['prɒdʒekt] *n.* 项目	perfect	['pɜːfɪkt] *adj.* 完美的
	[prə'dʒekt] *v.* 投掷		[pə'fekt] *v.* 使完善
contest	['kɒntest] *n.* 比赛	contrast	['kɒntrɑːst] *n.* 差别；差异
	[kən'test] *v.* 提出异议		[kən'trɑːst] *v.* 对照；对比
object	['ɒbdʒɪkt] *n.* 物质	estimate	['estɪmət] *n.* 估计；估价
	[əb'dʒekt] *v.* 反对		['estɪmeɪt] *v.* 估算
house	[haʊs] *n.* 住宅	excuse	[ɪk'skjuːs] *n.* 借口；理由
	[haʊz] *v.* 为…提供住宅		[ɪk'skjuːz] *v.* 原谅
use	[juːs] *n.* 用途	close	[kləʊs] *n.* 结束
	[juːz] *v.* 使用		[kləʊz] *v.* 关闭
minute	['mɪnɪt] *n.* 分钟	lead	[led] *n.* 铅
	[maɪ'njuːt] *adj.* 微小的；少量的		[liːd] *v.* 领导
live	[laɪv] *adj.* 活的	wind	[wɪnd] *n.* 风
	[lɪv] *v.* 生活		[waɪnd] *v.* 缠绕
wound	[wuːnd] *n.* 伤口	tear	[tɪə(r)] *n.* 泪水
	[waʊnd] *v.* 使受伤		[teə(r)] *v.* 撕碎

二 同音异形词

　　和汉语一样，英语中也有很多发音相同但是拼写不同的单词，叫作同音异形词。同音异形词在听力中会给考生造成一定的困扰，此时需要根据语境来选择合适的单词作答。积累同音异形词可以帮助考生扩大词汇量，还有助于考生提高听力水平。在完成答题后，也可以在检查答案时根据空格的前后文判断所填写单词是否正确。例如，剑 5–Test 1–Part 2 的第 12 题，brakes 和 breaks 是同音异形词，但是考生可以根据答案定位句"The only problem with this cot was that it had no brakes."来判断答案应该是 brakes。原文提到的是婴儿床的问题，而 breaks 指"休息"，含义不符合题目叙述。

以下词汇需重点掌握

音标	单词及释义	音标	单词及释义
[ˈɔːltə(r)]	alter v. 改变；改动 altar n. 祭坛；圣坛	[beə(r)]	bare adj. 光秃的 bear n. 熊 v. 承受
[ˈbærən]	baron n. 男爵 barren adj. 贫瘠的	[baʊ]	bough n. 大树枝 bow v. 点头；鞠躬
[breɪk]	brake n. 刹车 v. 刹车 break n. 休息 v. 破坏	[bred]	bred v. 饲养；培育（breed 的过去式和过去分词） bread n. 面包
[baɪ]	buy v. 购买 by prep. 通过	[sel]	sell v. 售卖 cell n. 细胞；小牢房；电池
[saɪt]	cite v. 引用；引证 sight n. 视力；看见 site n. 位置	[kɔːs]	coarse adj. 粗劣的 course n. 课程
[ˈkaʊns(ə)lə]	councilor n. 议员 counselor n. 顾问	[dæm]	dam n. 大坝 damn v. 咒骂；谴责
[dɪˈzɜːt]	desert v. 抛弃 dessert n. 甜点	[daɪ]	dye n. 染料 die v. 死亡
[feə(r)]	fair adj. 公正的 fare n. 车费	[ˈflaʊə(r)]	flour n. 面粉 flower n. 花朵
[gəˈrɪlə]	gorilla n. 大猩猩 guerrilla n. 游击队员	[hiːl]	heal v. 治愈 heel n. 脚后跟
[həʊl]	hole n. 洞 whole adj. 整体的	[aɪl]	isle n. 岛 aisle n. 过道
[naɪt]	night n. 晚上 knight n. 骑士	[piːs]	peace n. 和平 piece n. 片；张

音标	单词及释义	音标	单词及释义
[preɪ]	pray v. 祈祷 prey n. 猎物	[rəʊl]	role n. 角色 roll v. 滚动
[seɪl]	sail v. 航行 sale n. 出售	[sent]	scent n. 气味 cent n. 分
[ʃɪə(r)]	shear v. 剪切 sheer v. 偏航	[steə(r)]	stair n. 楼梯 stare v. 瞪
[teɪl]	tail n. 尾巴 tale n. 故事	[veɪn]	vain adj. 徒劳的 vein n. 静脉
['stɔːri]	story n. 故事 storey n. 楼层		

发音相近词

英语中一些发音相近的单词在听力考试中容易造成干扰，拼写也易混淆，进而影响对所听内容的判断及拼写。

以下词汇需重点掌握

单词	音标及释义	单词	音标及释义
abroad	[ə'brɔːd] adv. 在国外	allusion	[ə'luːʒn] n. 暗示
aboard	[ə'bɔːd] adv. 在（船、车、飞机）上	illusion	[ɪ'luːʒn] n. 幻觉
adapt	[ə'dæpt] v. 适应	amend	[ə'mend] v. 改正；修正
adopt	[ə'dɒpt] v. 采用	emend	[i'mend] v. 校正
adept	['ædept] n. 内行；专家	amoral	[,eɪ'mɒrəl] adj. 不分是非的
affect	[ə'fekt] v. 影响；假装	immoral	[ɪ'mɒrəl] adj. 不道德的
effect	[ɪ'fekt] n. 结果；影响	angel	['eɪndʒl] n. 天使
		angle	['æŋgl] n. 角度

单词	音标及释义	单词	音标及释义
ardour	[ˈɑːdə(r)] n. 热情	baggage	[ˈbægɪdʒ] n. 行李
adore	[əˈdɔː(r)] v. 崇拜	luggage	[ˈlʌgɪdʒ] n. 行李
adorn	[əˈdɔːn] v. 装饰	beam	[biːm] n. 梁; 光束
area	[ˈeəriə] n. 区域	bean	[biːn] n. 豆
era	[ˈɪərə] n. 时代	blade	[bleɪd] n. 刀刃
assemble	[əˈsembl] v. 集合; 装配	bald	[bɔːld] adj. 秃的
assembly	[əˈsembli] n. 集会; 装配	bold	[bəuld] adj. 大胆的
resemble	[rɪˈzembl] v. 像, 类似于	bloom	[bluːm] n. 开花
assent	[əˈsent] n. 同意	blossom	[ˈblɒsəm] n. 花朵
ascent	[əˈsent] n. 上升	blush	[blʌʃ] v. 脸红
accent	[ˈæksent] n. 口音	flush	[flʌʃ] v. 发红; 脸红
assume	[əˈsjuːm] v. 假定	flesh	[fleʃ] n. 肉; 肉体
resume	[rɪˈzjuːm] v. 恢复	flash	[flæʃ] n. 闪光
assure	[əˈʃuə(r)] v. 保证	bride	[braɪd] n. 新娘
ensure	[ɪnˈʃuə(r)] v. 使确定	bribe	[braɪb] n. 贿赂
insure	[ɪnˈʃuə(r)] v. 投保	brown	[braun] n. 棕色
attain	[əˈteɪn] v. 达到	brow	[brau] n. 眼眉
obtain	[əbˈteɪn] v. 获得	blow	[bləu] v. 吹
abstain	[əbˈsteɪn] v. 弃权; 离开	bullet	[ˈbulɪt] n. 子弹
aerial	[ˈeəriəl] adj. 空中的	bulletin	[ˈbulətɪn] n. 公告
oral	[ˈɔːrəl] adj. 口头的	carton	[ˈkɑːtn] n. 纸箱
award	[əˈwɔːd] v. 授予	cartoon	[kɑːˈtuːn] n. 动画片
reward	[rɪˈwɔːd] v. 奖赏	champion	[ˈtʃæmpiən] n. 冠军
badge	[bædʒ] n. 徽章	champagne	[ʃæmˈpeɪn] n. 香槟酒
bandage	[ˈbændɪdʒ] n. 绷带	campaign	[kæmˈpeɪn] n. 战役

单词	音标及释义	单词	音标及释义
chicken	['tʃɪkɪn] n. 鸡	counsel	['kaʊnsl] n. 忠告
kitchen	['kɪtʃɪn] n. 厨房	consul	['kɒnsl] n. 领事
chivalry	['ʃɪvəlri] n. 骑士精神	crayon	['kreɪən] n. 蜡笔
cavalry	['kævlri] n. 骑兵	canyon	['kænjən] n. 峡谷
chore	[tʃɔː(r)] n. 家务活	crow	[krəʊ] n. 乌鸦
chord	[kɔːd] n. 和弦	crown	[kraʊn] n. 王冠
cord	[kɔːd] n. 细绳	clown	[klaʊn] n. 小丑
clash	[klæʃ] n. (金属) 撞击声	cow	[kaʊ] n. 奶牛
crash	[kræʃ] n. 撞车；坠落	dairy	['deəri] n. 乳制品
collar	['kɒlə(r)] n. 领子	diary	['daɪəri] n. 日记
cellar	['selə(r)] n. 地窖	extensive	[ɪk'stensɪv] adj. 广泛的
colour	['kʌlə(r)] n. 颜色	intensive	[ɪn'tensɪv] adj. 加强的
confidant	['kɒnfɪdænt] n. 知己	faint	[feɪnt] v. 晕倒
confident	['kɒnfɪdənt] adj. 自信的	fate	[feɪt] v. 注定
contact	['kɒntækt] n. 接触	floor	[flɔː(r)] n. 地板
contract	['kɒntrækt] n. 合同	flour	['flaʊə(r)] n. 面粉
contrast	['kɒntrɑːst] n. 对比	gasp	[gɑːsp] v. 喘气
contend	[kən'tend] v. 主张；斗争	grasp	[grɑːsp] v. 抓住
content	['kɒntent] n. 内容；满足	glide	[glaɪd] v. 滑翔；滑行
context	['kɒntekst] n. 上下文	slide	[slaɪd] v. 使滑行
contest	['kɒntest] n. 竞争，比赛	slip	[slɪp] v. 滑倒
contort	[kən'tɔːt] v. 扭曲	grim	[grɪm] adj. 严酷的
distort	[dɪ'stɔːt] v. 歪曲	grime	[graɪm] n. 污点
retort	[rɪ'tɔːt] v. 反驳	growl	[graʊl] v. 咆哮
costume	['kɒstjuːm] n. 服装	howl	[haʊl] v. 长嚎
custom	['kʌstəm] n. 习惯		

单词	音标及释义	单词	音标及释义
hangar	['hæŋə(r)] n. 飞机库	latitude	['lætɪtjuːd] n. 纬度
hunger	['hʌŋgə(r)] n. 饥饿	altitude	['æltɪtjuːd] n. 高度
hotel	[həʊ'tel] n. 酒店	gratitude	['grætɪtjuːd] n. 感激
hostel	['hɒstl] n. 青年旅社	literacy	['lɪtərəsi] n. 读写能力
idle	['aɪdl] adj. 空闲的；懒惰的	literary	['lɪtərəri] adj. 文学的
ideal	[aɪ'diːəl] adj. 理想的	literature	['lɪtrətʃə(r)] n. 文学
immoral	[ɪ'mɒrəl] adj. 不道德的	literal	['lɪtərəl] adj. 字面意义的
immortal	[ɪ'mɔːtl] adj. 不朽的	lone	[ləʊn] adj. 独自的
incident	['ɪnsɪdənt] n. 事件	alone	[ə'ləʊn] adj. 单独的
accident	['æksɪdənt] n. 意外	lonely	['ləʊnli] adj. 孤独的
induce	[ɪn'djuːs] v. 促使；引诱	march	[mɑːtʃ] n. 三月（March）；前进
deduce	[dɪ'djuːs] v. 推测	match	[mætʃ] n. 比赛
reduce	[rɪ'djuːs] v. 减少	mission	['mɪʃn] n. 使命
seduce	[sɪ'djuːs] v. 引诱	emission	[ɪ'mɪʃn] n. 散发；发射
inspiration	[ˌɪnspə'reɪʃn] n. 灵感	mansion	['mænʃn] n. 大厦
aspiration	[ˌæspə'reɪʃn] n. 渴望	mortal	['mɔːtl] adj. 终将死亡的
intrude	[ɪn'truːd] v. 入侵	metal	['metl] n. 金属
extrude	[ɪk'struːd] v. 逐出	mental	['mentl] adj. 精神的
lapse	[læps] v. 流逝	medal	['medl] n. 勋章
elapse	[ɪ'læps] v. 消逝	model	['mɒdl] n. 模特
eclipse	[ɪ'klɪps] n. 日食	meddle	['medl] v. 干涉
later	['leɪtə(r)] adv. 后来	pat	[pæt] v. 轻拍
latter	['lætə(r)] adj. 后面的	tap	[tæp] v. 轻打
latest	['leɪtɪst] adj. 最近的	patent	['pætnt] n. 专利
lately	['leɪtli] adv. 最近	potent	['pəʊtnt] adj. 有力的

单词	音标及释义	单词	音标及释义
personnel	[ˌpɜːsəˈnel] n. 全体人员	require	[rɪˈkwaɪə(r)] v. 需要
personal	[ˈpɜːsənl] adj. 个人的	inquire	[ɪnˈkwaɪə(r)] v. 询问
phrase	[freɪz] n. 短语	acquire	[əˈkwaɪə(r)] v. 获得
phase	[feɪz] n. 阶段	revenge	[rɪˈvendʒ] v. 报仇
police	[pəˈliːs] n. 警察	avenge	[əˈvendʒ] v. 为…报仇
policy	[ˈpɒləsi] n. 政策	rip	[rɪp] v. 撕破
politics	[ˈpɒlətɪks] n. 政治	ripe	[raɪp] adj. 成熟的
precede	[prɪˈsiːd] v. 先于	rude	[ruːd] adj. 粗鲁的
proceed	[prəˈsiːd] v. 进行；继续	crude	[kruːd] adj. 天然的
principal	[ˈprɪnsəpl] adj. 首要的	scare	[skeə(r)] v. 使惊恐
printable	[ˈprɪntəbl] adj. 适宜刊印的	scarce	[skeəs] adj. 缺乏的
prospect	[ˈprɒspekt] n. 前景	socks	[sɒks] n. 短袜（sock 的复数）
perspective	[pəˈspektɪv] n. 视角	stocking	[ˈstɒkɪŋ] n. 长筒袜
protest	[prəˈtest] v. 抗议	source	[sɔːs] n. 来源
protect	[prəˈtekt] v. 保护	sauce	[sɔːs] n. 酱
purpose	[ˈpɜːpəs] n. 目的	saucer	[ˈsɔːsə(r)] n. 茶托
propose	[prəˈpəʊz] v. 建议	resource	[rɪˈsɔːs] n. 资源
quite	[kwaɪt] adv. 相当	recourse	[rɪˈkɔːs] n. 求援
quiet	[ˈkwaɪət] adj. 安静的	statue	[ˈstætʃuː] n. 塑像
recent	[ˈriːsnt] adj. 最近的	statute	[ˈstætʃuːt] n. 法令
resent	[rɪˈzent] v. 怨恨	status	[ˈsteɪtəs] n. 地位
reject	[rɪˈdʒekt] v. 拒绝	stripe	[straɪp] n. 条纹
eject	[ɪˈdʒekt] v. 逐出	strip	[strɪp] n. 条，带
inject	[ɪnˈdʒekt] v. 注射	trip	[trɪp] n. 旅行

单词	音标及释义	单词	音标及释义
strive	[straɪv] v. 努力	vision	['vɪʒn] n. 视觉
stride	[straɪd] v. 大步走	version	['vɜːʃn] n. 版本
suite	[swiːt] n. 宾馆套房	vocation	[vəʊ'keɪʃn] n. 职业
suit	[suːt] n. 西装，套装	vacation	[veɪ'keɪʃn] n. 假期
sweet	[swiːt] adj. 甜的	widow	['wɪdəʊ] n. 寡妇
sweat	[swet] n. 汗水	window	['wɪndəʊ] n. 窗户
tax	[tæks] n. 税		
taxi	['tæksi] n. 出租车		

四 英、美式拼写

英式英语和美式英语在拼写上有许多不同。英式英语多会保留来源语言的拼写方式，比如法语；而美式英语为了正确反映单词的实际发音，对拼写进行调整。英式英语和美式英语中单词拼写的差异主要体现在结尾处，比如英式以 -re 结尾，美式以 -er 结尾；英式以 -our 结尾，美式以 -or 结尾。

雅思听力考试中，在书写填空题答案时，考生既可以使用英式拼写，也可以使用美式拼写。书写正确的情况下，两种写法都可以得分，建议考生在整个听力考试中英美拼写选择一种并保持一致。比如剑 9-Test 2-Part 1 第 7 题答案为 theatre/theater，剑 16-Test 2-Part 1 的第 5 题答案为 colour/color，剑 17-Test 3-Part 4 的第 40 题答案为 litre/liter。

常见英美式拼写单词

1. 英式拼写以 -re 结尾，美式拼写以 -er 结尾。如下方示例：

英式拼写	美式拼写	单词释义
centre	center	中心
fibre	fiber	纤维

英式拼写	美式拼写	单词释义
litre	liter	升
theatre	theater	剧院
metre	meter	米

2. 英式拼写以 -our 结尾，美式拼写以 -or 结尾。如下方示例：

英式拼写	美式拼写	单词释义
colour	color	颜色
flavour	flavor	口味
humour	humor	幽默
labour	labor	劳动
neighbour	neighbor	邻居
favourite	favorite	最喜欢的
ardour	ardor	热情
clamour	clamor	喧哗
endeavour	endeavor	努力
rigour	rigor	严厉
rumour	rumor	谣言
savour	savor	品味
vigour	vigor	活力
tumour	tumor	肿瘤
harbour	harbor	港口

3. 英式拼写 -ise 结尾，美式拼写以 -ize 结尾。如下方示例：

英式拼写	美式拼写	单词释义
apologise	apologize	道歉
authorise	authorize	授权
fertilise	fertilize	施肥
memorise	memorize	记住
publicise	publicize	宣传
organise	organize	组织
recognise	recognize	认出
materialise	materialize	物化
neutralise	neutralize	使…中和
industrialise	industrialize	工业化

4. 英式拼写以 -yse 结尾，美式拼写以 -yze 结尾。如下方示例：

英式拼写	美式拼写	单词释义
analyse	analyze	分析
paralyse	paralyze	使瘫痪或麻痹
catalyse	catalyze	催化

5. 英式拼写中，动词以元音＋字母 l 结尾时，如果在结尾再添加元音，则双写 l；美式拼写无须双写。如下方示例：

英式拼写	美式拼写	单词释义
travelled	traveled	旅游
fuelled	fueled	给…提供燃料

英式拼写	美式拼写	单词释义
controlled	controled	控制
pedalled	pedaled	踩踏板
channelled	channeled	输送
cancelled	canceled	取消

6. 英式拼写以 -ence 结尾，美式拼写以 -ense 结尾。如下方示例：

英式拼写	美式拼写	单词释义
defence	defense	防卫
licence	license	执照
offence	offense	冒犯
pretence	pretense	借口

7. 英式拼写以 -ogue 结尾，美式拼写以 -og 或 -ogue 结尾均可。如下方示例：

英式拼写	美式拼写	单词释义
catalogue	catalog/catalogue	目录
analogue	analog/analogue	相似物
dialogue	dialog/dialogue	对话
travelogue	travelog/travelogue	旅行纪录片

8. 英式拼写结尾处 e 前面双写辅音字母，美式拼写通常不保留最后的辅音和 e。如下方示例：

英式拼写	美式拼写	单词释义
programme	program	项目
kilogramme	kilogram	千克
gramme	gram	克

五 连字符

英语中的连字符有两大功能：第一个功能是用于移行，把不在同一行的某个单词连接起来；第二是把两个或者两个以上的单词连接起来，构成新词。雅思听力主要考查连字符的第二个功能。连字符常用在作为定语的一个单元修饰语之间，以避免歧义。例如，a small business man（一位个子矮小的商人）和 a small-business man（一个做小本生意的人）。

另外，连字符还可以用在位于名词之前的复合修饰语之间。例如：Jim is a 15-year-old boy.（Jim 是一个 15 岁的男孩。）最后，在 self-、ex-、half-、quarter-、all- 作为词缀的各部分之间应该加连字符。

具体情况可以参考以下真题示例：

剑 6–Test 1–Part 1 中的第 1 题：We do have a keep-fit studio（健身工作室）.

剑 7–Test 1–Part 1 中的第 4 题：It's a door-to-door service（上门服务）and it would suit you much better...

剑 7–Test 2–Part 2 中的第 18 题：The most exciting place to visit is the new Entertainment Complex with seven-screen cinema（带七块银幕的电影院）.

剑 10–Test 2–Part 4 中的第 40 题：Instead, more and more people are becoming self-employed（自由职业的）.

以下表达需要重点掌握

long-distance telephone 长途电话	old-style machine 旧式机器
face-to-face interview 面对面采访	door-to-door service 上门服务
brother-in-law 妹夫；姐夫；小叔子；小舅子	peace-loving people 热爱和平的人
self-employed worker 个体经营者	medium-sized man 中等身材的男人
highly-developed industry 高度发达的工业	hand-made goods 手工制品
hard-working employee 勤劳的员工	man-made lake 人工湖
full-time job 全职工作	part-time job 兼职工作
low-risk investment 低风险投资	keep-fit studio 健身房

first-aid kit 急救箱

funny-looking man 相貌可笑的男人

a 5-year-old boy 一个 5 岁的小男孩

self-respect 自尊心

X-ray X 光

cold-blooded animal 冷血动物

well-dressed 穿着讲究的

self-control 自控力

half-asleep 半睡半醒的

U-turn 掉头，U 型转弯

六 缩写

雅思听力填空题一般不会出现单词缩写，但了解常见缩写有助于考生更好地理解题目要求和听力关键信息。例如题干要求中经常出现的 NB，全称为 nota bene，是一个拉丁文短语，意为 note well。动词 nota 是 notare 的单数派生词，意为 to note，通常缩写为 NB。NB 用于强调，引导考生在阅读下面的材料时要特别注意。NB 是法律文件、学术论文、数学中的常见缩写。在剑 8–Test 1–Part 1 第 10 题的题干中出现了 NB，听力原文中用 "Look!" 来表达，二者的强调作用一致。

以下缩写需重点掌握

缩写	全称	单词释义
NB	nota bene	注意
a.m.	ante meridiem	上午
p.m.	post meridiem	下午
ATM	Automated Teller Machine	自动取款机
GPS	Global Positioning System	全球定位系统
POS	Point of Sales	刷卡机
IT	Information Technology	信息技术
PDF	Portable Document Format	便携文档格式

缩写	全称	单词释义
A.D.	Anno Domini	公元
BC	Before Christ	公元前
CV	curriculum vitae	简历
Ph.D	Doctor of Philosophy	博士学位
CC.	Carbon Copy	抄送
BBQ	barbecue	烧烤
APEC	Asia-Pacific Economic Cooperation	亚太经贸合作组织
CEO	Chief Executive Officer	首席执行官
CPU	Central Processing Unit	中央处理器
DIY	do it yourself	自己动手
EU	European Union	欧洲联盟
IQ	Intelligence Quotient	智商
MBA	Master of Business Administration	工商管理硕士
UFO	Unknown/Unidentified Flying Object	不明飞行物
UNESCO	United Nations Educational, Scientific and Cultural Organization	联合国教科文组织
UPS	United Parcel Service	美国联合包裹运送服务公司
WTO	World Trade Organization	世界贸易组织

第三节　高频考点词

　　本节收录的雅思真题考点词取自过去 4 年约 400 场真实的雅思听力考试，这些考试场次是完全连贯的，考试的素材也比较完整，对还原雅思考试最重要的考点词具有比较强的确定性。雅思考试本身属于题库制的考试，因此本章的学习对考生今后会在考场上遇到哪些考点词提供了非常重要的参考依据。本节收录的考点词筛选过程如下：

　　1 从考试真题的题干、选项以及对应的原文答案句超过 10,000 个单词中初步筛选出 6,000 个左右的重点词汇。

　　2 对这些词汇进行合并。例如将 vanish 与 vanishing、vanished 进行合并，将 predator 与 predators 进行合并。

　　3 按照单词出现的频次从高到低排序。例如 donation、helicopter 都出现 9 次，将它们排列在一起。而 library、sculpture 出现 8 次，则排在后面。因此越靠前的单词在考试中出现频率越高。

　　4 按照词性进行归类，方便考生分类学习。本节共选取了 843 个单数名词、260 个复数名词、183 个动词、290 个形容词、53 个副词、100 组搭配和常见地名。

　　5 对于出现频率相同的单词，按照"答案词优先"原则，在排序上把考试中作为答案词出现的单词排在前面，把作为题干词出现的排在后面。

　　由于是听力词汇，因此在本节的学习中，需要重点关注能否通过音频、通过听到的方式识别这些单词，同时需要格外注意单词的拼写。完成本节的学习后，可以用练习册中对应的练习进行听写训练。

information	[ˌɪnfəˈmeɪʃn] n. 信息	desert	[ˈdezət] n. 沙漠
museum	[mjuˈziːəm] n. 博物馆	environment	[ɪnˈvaɪrənmənt] n. 环境
research	[ˈriːsɜːtʃ] n. 研究	fishing	[ˈfɪʃɪŋ] n. 渔业；捕鱼
certificate	[səˈtɪfɪkət] n. 证书	manager	[ˈmænɪdʒə(r)] n. 经理；管理人员
company	[ˈkʌmpəni] n. 公司		
exhibition	[ˌeksɪˈbɪʃn] n. 展览	reception	[rɪˈsepʃn] n. 接待；接收
insurance	[ɪnˈʃʊərəns] n. 保险	attitude	[ˈætɪtjuːd] n. 态度
hotel	[həʊˈtel] n. 旅馆	balcony	[ˈbælkəni] n. 阳台
building	[ˈbɪldɪŋ] n. 建筑	contact	[ˈkɒntækt] n. 接触；联系
discount	[ˈdɪskaʊnt] n. 折扣	donation	[dəʊˈneɪʃn] n. 捐赠
electricity	[ɪˌlekˈtrɪsəti] n. 电流	helicopter	[ˈhelɪkɒptə(r)] n. 直升机
family	[ˈfæməli] n. 家庭；亲属	impact	[ˈɪmpækt] n. 影响；撞击
equipment	[ɪˈkwɪpmənt] n. 设备	kitchen	[ˈkɪtʃɪn] n. 厨房
garage	[ˈɡærɑːʒ] n. 车库；修理厂	membership	[ˈmembəʃɪp] n. 会员资格
location	[ləʊˈkeɪʃn] n. 位置	newspaper	[ˈnjuːzpeɪpə(r)] n. 报纸
display	[dɪˈspleɪ] n. 显示；展出	plastic	[ˈplæstɪk] n. 塑料
government	[ˈɡʌvənmənt] n. 政府	reference	[ˈrefrəns] n. 参考；涉及
parking	[ˈpɑːkɪŋ] n. 停车	temperature	[ˈtemprətʃə(r)] n. 温度
training	[ˈtreɪnɪŋ] n. 训练	transport	[ˈtrænspɔːt] n. 交通；运输
website	[ˈwebsaɪt] n. 网站	climate	[ˈklaɪmət] n. 气候
deposit	[dɪˈpɒzɪt] n. 押金；沉淀物	library	[ˈlaɪbrəri] n. 图书馆

photograph	['fəʊtəgrɑːf] n. 照片	energy	['enədʒi] n. 能量
requirement	[rɪ'kwaɪəmənt] n. 要求；必要条件	feature	['fiːtʃə(r)] n. 特征
		handle	['hændl] n. 把手；柄
sculpture	['skʌlptʃə(r)] n. 雕塑	passport	['pɑːspɔːt] n. 护照
traffic	['træfɪk] n. 交通	performance	[pə'fɔːməns] n. 表现
accommodation	[ə,kɒmə'deɪʃn] n. 住处	pollution	[pə'luːʃn] n. 污染
airport	['eəpɔːt] n. 机场	project	['prɒdʒekt] n. 计划；项目
centre	['sentə(r)] n. 中心	report	[rɪ'pɔːt] n. 报告
feedback	['fiːdbæk] n. 反馈	salary	['sæləri] n. 工资
furniture	['fɜːnɪtʃə(r)] n. 家具	scheme	[skiːm] n. 计划
hospital	['hɒspɪtl] n. 医院	theatre	['θɪətə(r)] n. 电影院；剧院；露天剧场
labour	['leɪbə(r)] n. 劳动力		
methodology	[,meθə'dɒlədʒi] n. 方法论	audience	['ɔːdiəns] n. 观众；听众
painting	['peɪntɪŋ] n. 绘画；油画	background	['bækgraʊnd] n. 背景
presentation	[,prezn'teɪʃn] n. 展示	bottle	['bɒtl] n. 瓶子
program	['prəʊgræm] n. 程序；计划	cafeteria	[,kæfə'tɪəriə] n. 自助餐厅
qualification	[,kwɒlɪfɪ'keɪʃn] n. 资格	cinema	['sɪnəmə] n. 电影院
relationship	[rɪ'leɪʃnʃɪp] n. 关系	competition	[,kɒmpə'tɪʃn] n. 竞争；比赛
science	['saɪəns] n. 科学	concentration	[,kɒnsn'treɪʃn] n. 集中；专心
technology	[tek'nɒlədʒi] n. 技术	culture	['kʌltʃə(r)] n. 文化
village	['vɪlɪdʒ] n. 村庄	decoration	[,dekə'reɪʃn] n. 装饰
damage	['dæmɪdʒ] n. 损害	development	[dɪ'veləpmənt] n. 发展；开发
disease	[dɪ'ziːz] n. 疾病	device	[dɪ'vaɪs] n. 设备

engineer	[ˌendʒɪˈnɪə(r)] n. 工程师	advice	[ədˈvaɪs] n. 建议
entertainment	[ˌentəˈteɪnmənt] n. 娱乐	agriculture	[ˈæɡrɪkʌltʃə(r)] n. 农业
experience	[ɪkˈspɪəriəns] n. 经验; 经历	architecture	[ˈɑːkɪtektʃə(r)] n. 建筑
gender	[ˈdʒendə(r)] n. 性别	benefit	[ˈbenɪfɪt] n. 益处
helmet	[ˈhelmɪt] n. 头盔	budget	[ˈbʌdʒɪt] n. 预算
hunting	[ˈhʌntɪŋ] n. 打猎	carbon	[ˈkɑːbən] n. 碳
income	[ˈɪnkʌm] n. 收入	castle	[ˈkɑːsl] n. 城堡
instrument	[ˈɪnstrəmənt] n. 仪器; 乐器	cement	[sɪˈment] n. 水泥
language	[ˈlæŋɡwɪdʒ] n. 语言	cheese	[tʃiːz] n. 奶酪
material	[məˈtɪəriəl] n. 材料	chocolate	[ˈtʃɒklət] n. 巧克力
microwave	[ˈmaɪkrəweɪv] n. 微波; 微波炉	commodity	[kəˈmɒdəti] n. 商品
		communication	[kəˌmjuːnɪˈkeɪʃn] n. 沟通; 通信
playground	[ˈpleɪɡraʊnd] n. 操场		
pottery	[ˈpɒtəri] n. 陶器	confidence	[ˈkɒnfɪdəns] n. 信心
rainfall	[ˈreɪnfɔːl] n. 降雨; 降雨量	cottage	[ˈkɒtɪdʒ] n. 村舍
registration	[ˌredʒɪˈstreɪʃn] n. 登记; 注册	cotton	[ˈkɒtn] n. 棉花
sailing	[ˈseɪlɪŋ] n. 帆船; 航行	credit	[ˈkredɪt] n. 信用; 学分
shower	[ˈʃaʊə(r)] n. 淋浴	current	[ˈkʌrənt] n. 水流; 趋势
square	[skweə(r)] n. 广场; 正方形	definition	[ˌdefɪˈnɪʃn] n. 定义
university	[ˌjuːnɪˈvɜːsəti] n. 大学	delivery	[dɪˈlɪvəri] n. 交付
volunteer	[ˌvɒlənˈtɪə(r)] n. 志愿者	director	[dəˈrektə(r)] n. 主任; 导演
waterfall	[ˈwɔːtəfɔːl] n. 瀑布	efficiency	[ɪˈfɪʃnsi] n. 效率
wildlife	[ˈwaɪldlaɪf] n. 野生动物	employee	[ɪmˈplɔɪiː] n. 雇员

entrance	['entrəns] n. 入口	protection	[prə'tekʃn] n. 保护
evolution	[ˌiːvə'luːʃn] n. 进化	publicity	[pʌb'lɪsəti] n. 宣传；公开
experiment	[ɪk'sperɪmənt] n. 实验	quality	['kwɒləti] n. 质量；特性
fertilizer	['fɜːtəlaɪzə(r)] n. 肥料	questionnaire	[ˌkwestʃə'neə(r)] n. 问卷
fridge	[frɪdʒ] n. 电冰箱	reaction	[ri'ækʃn] n. 反应
identity	[aɪ'dentəti] n. 身份；同一性	reputation	[ˌrepju'teɪʃn] n. 名声
interaction	[ˌɪntər'ækʃn] n. 相互作用；交流	restaurant	['restrɒnt] n. 餐馆
introduction	[ˌɪntrə'dʌkʃn] n. 介绍；引进	safety	['seɪfti] n. 安全
		security	[sɪ'kjʊərəti] n. 安全
island	['aɪlənd] n. 岛	silver	['sɪlvə(r)] n. 银
landscape	['lændskeɪp] n. 风景	survey	['sɜːveɪ] n. 调查
mountain	['maʊntən] n. 山；山脉	technician	[tek'nɪʃn] n. 技术员
observation	[ˌɒbzə'veɪʃn] n. 观察	textile	['tekstaɪl] n. 纺织品
occupation	[ˌɒkju'peɪʃn] n. 职业	ability	[ə'bɪləti] n. 能力
option	['ɒpʃn] n. 选项	achievement	[ə'tʃiːvmənt] n. 成就
partner	['pɑːtnə(r)] n. 伙伴；合伙人	action	['ækʃn] n. 行动
payment	['peɪmənt] n. 付款	advantage	[əd'vɑːntɪdʒ] n. 优点
perfume	['pɜːfjuːm] n. 香水；香味	agency	['eɪdʒənsi] n. 代理；中介
population	[ˌpɒpju'leɪʃn] n. 人口	alternative	[ɔːl'tɜːnətɪv] n. 可选择的事物
postcode	['pəʊstkəʊd] n. 邮政编码		
priority	[praɪ'ɒrəti] n. 优先	appearance	[ə'pɪərəns] n. 外貌；外观
prison	['prɪzn] n. 监狱	application	[ˌæplɪ'keɪʃn] n. 应用；申请
professor	[prə'fesə(r)] n. 教授	architect	['ɑːkɪtekt] n. 建筑师

assessment	[əˈsesmənt] *n.* 评价	content	[ˈkɒntent] *n.* 内容；目录
author	[ˈɔːθə(r)] *n.* 作者	couple	[ˈkʌpl] *n.* 一对；夫妇
avenue	[ˈævənjuː] *n.* 大街	cousin	[ˈkʌzn] *n.* 同辈表亲（或堂亲）；远亲
bibliography	[ˌbɪbliˈɒgrəfi] *n.* 参考书目	dancing	[ˈdɑːnsɪŋ] *n.* 舞蹈
biology	[baɪˈɒlədʒi] *n.* 生物；生物学	database	[ˈdeɪtəbeɪs] *n.* 数据库
breakfast	[ˈbrekfəst] *n.* 早餐	deadline	[ˈdedlaɪn] *n.* 最终期限
buffet	[ˈbʌfeɪ] *n.* 自助餐	dentist	[ˈdentɪst] *n.* 牙科医生
camera	[ˈkæmrə] *n.* 照相机；摄影机	department	[dɪˈpɑːtmənt] *n.* 部门；系
campsite	[ˈkæmpsaɪt] *n.* 营地	description	[dɪˈskrɪpʃn] *n.* 描述
carving	[ˈkɑːvɪŋ] *n.* 雕刻	dinner	[ˈdɪnə(r)] *n.* 晚餐
ceremony	[ˈserəməni] *n.* 典礼，仪式	dinosaur	[ˈdaɪnəsɔː(r)] *n.* 恐龙
charge	[tʃɑːdʒ] *n.* 费用；电荷	discussion	[dɪˈskʌʃn] *n.* 讨论
climbing	[ˈklaɪmɪŋ] *n.* 攀爬	disturbance	[dɪˈstɜːbəns] *n.* 干扰
collection	[kəˈlekʃn] *n.* 收集；收藏品	diversity	[daɪˈvɜːsəti] *n.* 多样性
commerce	[ˈkɒmɜːs] *n.* 商业	drawback	[ˈdrɔːbæk] *n.* 缺点
committee	[kəˈmɪti] *n.* 委员会	education	[ˌedʒuˈkeɪʃn] *n.* 教育
conclusion	[kənˈkluːʒn] *n.* 结论	emotion	[ɪˈməʊʃn] *n.* 情感；情绪
condition	[kənˈdɪʃn] *n.* 条件；情况	engineering	[ˌendʒɪˈnɪərɪŋ] *n.* 工程；工程学
conservation	[ˌkɒnsəˈveɪʃn] *n.* 保存；保护	evidence	[ˈevɪdəns] *n.* 证据
construction	[kənˈstrʌkʃn] *n.* 建设	expansion	[ɪkˈspænʃn] *n.* 膨胀
consumption	[kənˈsʌmpʃn] *n.* 消费	expectation	[ˌekspekˈteɪʃn] *n.* 期待；预期
container	[kənˈteɪnə(r)] *n.* 容器		

footwear	['fʊtweə(r)] n. 鞋类	multimedia	[ˌmʌlti'miːdiə] n. 多媒体
format	['fɔːmæt] n. 格式	nature	['neɪtʃə(r)] n. 自然；性质
foundation	[faʊn'deɪʃn] n. 基础	nutrition	[njuˈtrɪʃn] n. 营养
frequency	['friːkwənsi] n. 频率	occupancy	['ɒkjəpənsi] n. 占有
insight	['ɪnsaɪt] n. 洞察力	package	['pækɪdʒ] n. 包裹
interpretation	[ɪnˌtɜːprəˈteɪʃn] n. 解释	password	['pɑːswɜːd] n. 密码
investment	[ɪn'vestmənt] n. 投资；投入	personality	[ˌpɜːsə'næləti] n. 个性
irrigation	[ˌɪrɪ'geɪʃn] n. 灌溉	petrol	['petrəl] n. 汽油
journalist	['dʒɜːnəlɪst] n. 新闻工作者	portion	['pɔːʃn] n. 部分
keyboard	['kiːbɔːd] n. 键盘	poverty	['pɒvəti] n. 贫穷
leaflet	['liːflət] n. 传单	predator	['predətə(r)] n. 捕食者
lecturer	['lektʃərə(r)] n. 讲师；演讲者	printer	['prɪntə(r)] n. 打印机
liquid	['lɪkwɪd] n. 液体	product	['prɒdʌkt] n. 产品；作品
locker	['lɒkə(r)] n. 存放室	protein	['prəʊtiːn] n. 蛋白质
lounge	[laʊndʒ] n. 休息室	recommendation	[ˌrekəmen'deɪʃn] n. 推荐；建议
majority	[mə'dʒɒrəti] n. 大多数		
manufacture	[ˌmænju'fæktʃə(r)] n. 制造	recreation	[ˌriːkri'eɪʃn] n. 娱乐
massage	['mæsɑːʒ] n. 按摩	regulation	[ˌregju'leɪʃn] n. 管理；规则
maximum	['mæksɪməm] n. 最大值	rubber	['rʌbə(r)] n. 橡胶
mechanism	['mekənɪzəm] n. 机制	screen	[skriːn] n. 屏幕
migration	[maɪ'greɪʃn] n. 迁移；移民	session	['seʃn] n. 部分
movement	['muːvmənt] n. 运动；活动	software	['sɒftweə(r)] n. 软件
		storage	['stɔːrɪdʒ] n. 存储；仓库

subject	['sʌbdʒɪkt] n. 主题；科目	association	[ə,səʊsi'eɪʃn] n. 协会；结合
suburb	['sʌbɜːb] n. 郊区	astronomy	[ə'strɒnəmi] n. 天文学
tablecloth	['teɪblklɒθ] n. 桌布	balance	['bæləns] n. 平衡
talent	['tælənt] n. 才能；天才	balloon	[bə'luːn] n. 气球
threat	[θret] n. 威胁	barbecue	['bɑːbɪkjuː] n. 烤肉
triangle	['traɪæŋgl] n. 三角形	baseball	['beɪsbɔːl] n. 棒球
tunnel	['tʌnl] n. 隧道	basement	['beɪsmənt] n. 地下室
turtle	['tɜːtl] n. 海龟	bathroom	['bɑːθrum] n. 浴室
uniform	['juːnɪfɔːm] n. 制服	bedroom	['bedrʊm] n. 卧室
unreliability	[,ʌnrɪ,laɪə'bɪləti] n. 不可靠	belief	[bɪ'liːf] n. 相信
warehouse	['weəhaʊs] n. 仓库	bicycle	['baɪsɪkl] n. 自行车
wedding	['wedɪŋ] n. 婚礼	biography	[baɪ'ɒgrəfi] n. 传记
weight	[weɪt] n. 重量	blanket	['blæŋkɪt] n. 毛毯
workforce	['wɜːkfɔːs] n. 劳动力	booklet	['bʊklət] n. 小册子
absence	['æbsəns] n. 缺席	branch	[brɑːntʃ] n. 分支
accident	['æksɪdənt] n. 事故；意外	breathing	['briːðɪŋ] n. 呼吸
advance	[əd'vɑːns] n. 发展	broadcast	['brɔːdkɑːst] n. 广播
advertisement	[əd'vɜːtɪsmənt] n. 广告	businessman	['bɪznəsmæn] n. 商人
advertising	['ædvətaɪzɪŋ] n. 广告；宣传	cabinet	['kæbɪnət] n. 橱柜
anxiety	[æŋ'zaɪəti] n. 焦虑	calculation	[,kælkju'leɪʃn] n. 计算
arrangement	[ə'reɪndʒmənt] n. 安排	calendar	['kælɪndə(r)] n. 日历；历法
assignment	[ə'saɪnmənt] n. 分配；作业	camp	[kæmp] n. 露营；营地

caravan	['kærəvæn] *n.* 大篷车	crocodile	['krɒkədaɪl] *n.* 鳄鱼
carpet	['kɑːpɪt] *n.* 地毯	customer	['kʌstəmə(r)] *n.* 顾客
celebration	[ˌselɪ'breɪʃn] *n.* 庆典；庆祝	danger	['deɪndʒə(r)] *n.* 危险
celebrity	[sə'lebrəti] *n.* 名人	departure	[dɪ'pɑːtʃə(r)] *n.* 离开；出发
century	['sentʃəri] *n.* 世纪	design	[dɪ'zaɪn] *n.* 设计
chairman	['tʃeəmən] *n.* 主席；董事长	destination	[ˌdestɪ'neɪʃn] *n.* 目的地
character	['kærəktə(r)] *n.* 性格；特性；角色	detail	['diːteɪl] *n.* 细节
chemist	['kemɪst] *n.* 化学家	dialogue	['daɪəlɒg] *n.* 对话
cheque	[tʃek] *n.* 支票	diploma	[dɪ'pləumə] *n.* 学位证书
citizen	['sɪtɪzn] *n.* 公民	direction	[də'rekʃn] *n.* 方向；指导
client	['klaɪənt] *n.* 客户	disability	[ˌdɪsə'bɪləti] *n.* 残疾；缺陷
combination	[ˌkɒmbɪ'neɪʃn] *n.* 结合	dissertation	[ˌdɪsə'teɪʃn] *n.* 论文
comment	['kɒment] *n.* 评论	document	['dɒkjumənt] *n.* 文档
community	[kə'mjuːnəti] *n.* 社区	dolphin	['dɒlfɪn] *n.* 海豚
computer	[kəm'pjuːtə(r)] *n.* 计算机	downhill	[ˌdaʊn'hɪl] *n.* 下坡
concert	['kɒnsət] *n.* 音乐会	duration	[dju'reɪʃn] *n.* 持续
consultant	[kən'sʌltənt] *n.* 顾问	eclipse	[ɪ'klɪps] *n.* 日食；月食
consumer	[kən'sjuːmə(r)] *n.* 消费者	economy	[ɪ'kɒnəmi] *n.* 经济
conversation	[ˌkɒnvə'seɪʃn] *n.* 对话	effect	[ɪ'fekt] *n.* 效果
cooking	['kʊkɪŋ] *n.* 烹饪	emission	[ɪ'mɪʃn] *n.* 发射
cooperation	[kəʊˌɒpə'reɪʃn] *n.* 合作	enlargement	[ɪn'lɑːdʒmənt] *n.* 放大
council	['kaʊnsl] *n.* 委员会	evaporation	[ɪˌvæpə'reɪʃn] *n.* 蒸发

exploration	[ˌeksplə'reɪʃn] n. 探测	installation	[ˌɪnstə'leɪʃn] n. 安装
explorer	[ɪk'splɔːrə(r)] n. 探险家	institute	['ɪnstɪtjuːt] n. 机构
fabric	['fæbrɪk] n. 织物	internship	['ɪntɜːnʃɪp] n. 实习生；实习
fossil	['fɒsl] n. 化石	interviewee	[ˌɪntəvjuː'iː] n. 受采访者；被面试者
fountain	['faʊntən] n. 喷泉；泉水		
friendship	['frendʃɪp] n. 友谊	investigation	[ɪnˌvestɪ'geɪʃn] n. 调查
function	['fʌŋkʃn] n. 功能	kidney	['kɪdni] n. 肾脏
funding	['fʌndɪŋ] n. 提供资金	knowledge	['nɒlɪdʒ] n. 知识
grocery	['grəʊsəri] n. 杂货店	laptop	['læptɒp] n. 笔记本电脑
harvest	['hɑːvɪst] n. 收获	layout	['leɪaʊt] n. 布局
headphone	['hedfəʊn] n. 耳机	leader	['liːdə(r)] n. 领导者
heater	['hiːtə(r)] n. 加热器	lecture	['lektʃə(r)] n. 演讲
horror	['hɒrə(r)] n. 惊恐	legislation	[ˌledʒɪs'leɪʃn] n. 立法；法律
identification	[aɪˌdentɪfɪ'keɪʃn] n. 识别；认同	license	['laɪsns] n. 执照，许可证
		lifestyle	['laɪfstaɪl] n. 生活方式
illustration	[ˌɪlə'streɪʃn] n. 说明；插图；例证	literature	['lɪtrətʃə(r)] n. 文学；文献
		loyalty	['lɔɪəlti] n. 忠诚
improvement	[ɪm'pruːvmənt] n. 进步	maintenance	['meɪntənəns] n. 维修；保持
incident	['ɪnsɪdənt] n. 事件	medication	[ˌmedɪ'keɪʃn] n. 药物；药物治疗
individual	[ˌɪndɪ'vɪdʒuəl] n. 个人		
infrastructure	['ɪnfrəstrʌktʃə(r)] n. 基础设施	member	['membə(r)] n. 成员；会员
		method	['meθəd] n. 方法
innovation	[ˌɪnə'veɪʃn] n. 创新	mirror	['mɪrə(r)] n. 镜子

mixture	['mɪkstʃə(r)] *n.* 混合；混合物	potential	[pə'tenʃl] *n.* 潜力；可能性
monitor	['mɒnɪtə(r)] *n.* 监视器	powder	['paʊdə(r)] *n.* 粉末
morality	[mə'ræləti] *n.* 道德；品行	preparation	[ˌprepə'reɪʃn] *n.* 预备；准备
mushroom	['mʌʃrʊm] *n.* 蘑菇	privacy	['prɪvəsi] *n.* 隐私
obligation	[ˌɒblɪ'geɪʃn] *n.* 义务；职责	promotion	[prə'məʊʃn] *n.* 晋升；推广
official	[ə'fɪʃl] *n.* 官员	psychology	[saɪ'kɒlədʒi] *n.* 心理学
organisation	[ˌɔ:gənaɪ'zeɪʃn] *n.* 组织	puzzle	['pʌzl] *n.* 谜；智力游戏
orientation	[ˌɔ:riən'teɪʃn] *n.* 方向	rainbow	['reɪnbəʊ] *n.* 彩虹
origin	['ɒrɪdʒɪn] *n.* 起源	reduction	[rɪ'dʌkʃn] *n.* 减少；下降
packaging	['pækɪdʒɪŋ] *n.* 包装	region	['ri:dʒən] *n.* 地区
participant	[pɑ:'tɪsɪpənt] *n.* 参与者	religion	[rɪ'lɪdʒən] *n.* 宗教
participation	[pɑ:ˌtɪsɪ'peɪʃn] *n.* 参与	renovation	[ˌrenə'veɪʃn] *n.* 革新
patience	['peɪʃns] *n.* 耐心	reproduction	[ˌri:prə'dʌkʃn] *n.* 繁殖；复制
penguin	['peŋgwɪn] *n.* 企鹅	request	[rɪ'kwest] *n.* 要求
pepper	['pepə(r)] *n.* 胡椒	researcher	[rɪ'sɜ:tʃə(r)] *n.* 研究员
period	['pɪəriəd] *n.* 时期	reservation	[ˌrezə'veɪʃn] *n.* 预约；保留
phenomenon	[fə'nɒmɪnən] *n.* 现象	resort	[rɪ'zɔ:t] *n.* 手段；度假地
picnic	['pɪknɪk] *n.* 野餐	respondent	[rɪ'spɒndənt] *n.* 应答者
plaster	['plɑ:stə(r)] *n.* 石膏	restoration	[ˌrestə'reɪʃn] *n.* 恢复
poetry	['pəʊətri] *n.* 诗歌	revenue	['revənju:] *n.* 财政收入
portrait	['pɔ:treɪt] *n.* 肖像；描写	review	[rɪ'vju:] *n.* 回顾；复习；评论
position	[pə'zɪʃn] *n.* 位置；职位	rubbish	['rʌbɪʃ] *n.* 垃圾

sandwich	['sænwɪdʒ] n. 三明治	treatment	['triːtmənt] n. 治疗
scenery	['siːnəri] n. 风景	twilight	['twaɪlaɪt] n. 黄昏
schedule	['ʃedjuːl] n. 时间表	underground	[ˌʌndə'graʊnd] n. 地铁
seafood	['siːfuːd] n. 海鲜	vacation	[veɪ'keɪʃn] n. 假期
seaweed	['siːwiːd] n. 海藻；海草	vegetarian	[ˌvedʒə'teəriən] n. 素食者
signal	['sɪgnəl] n. 信号	vehicle	['viːəkl] n. 车辆；工具
signature	['sɪgnətʃə(r)] n. 签名	vocabulary	[və'kæbjələri] n. 词汇；词汇量
souvenir	[ˌsuːvə'nɪə(r)] n. 纪念品		
stadium	['steɪdiəm] n. 体育场	volcano	[vɒl'keɪnəʊ] n. 火山
standard	['stændəd] n. 标准	waiter	['weɪtə(r)] n. 服务员
stomach	['stʌmək] n. 胃	warning	['wɔːnɪŋ] n. 警告
string	[strɪŋ] n. 线；一串	watering	['wɔːtə(r)] n. 浇水
studio	['stjuːdiəʊ] n. 工作室	waterproof	['wɔːtəpruːf] n. 防水材料
sunset	['sʌnset] n. 日落，傍晚	wealth	[welθ] n. 财富
supervisor	['suːpəvaɪzə(r)] n. 监督者	woodland	['wʊdlənd] n. 林地；森林
system	['sɪstəm] n. 系统；制度	worksheet	['wɜːkʃiːt] n. 工作表；练习题
teamwork	['tiːmwɜːk] n. 团队合作	workshop	['wɜːkʃɒp] n. 研讨会
telephone	['telɪfəʊn] n. 电话	writer	['raɪtə(r)] n. 作者
therapy	['θerəpi] n. 疗法	absorber	[əbzɔːbə(r)] n. 减震器；吸收器
timetable	['taɪmteɪbl] n. 时间表；计划		
tolerance	['tɒlərəns] n. 容忍	abstract	['æbstrækt] n. 摘要；抽象
tourism	['tʊərɪzəm] n. 旅游业	abstraction	[æb'strækʃn] n. 提取；抽象
		accuracy	['ækjərəsi] n. 准确度

acknowledgement	[əkˈnɒlɪdʒmənt] n. 承认	attraction	[əˈtrækʃn] n. 吸引
adaptation	[ˌædæpˈteɪʃn] n. 适应；改编	authority	[ɔːˈθɒrəti] n. 权威；当局
administration	[ədˌmɪnɪˈstreɪʃn] n. 管理；管理机构	authorization	[ˌɔːθəraɪˈzeɪʃn] n. 授权
		availability	[əˌveɪləˈbɪləti] n. 可用性
administrator	[ədˈmɪnɪstreɪtə(r)] n. 管理人	barcode	[ˈbɑːkəʊd] n. 条形码
allocation	[ˌæləˈkeɪʃn] n. 分配	battery	[ˈbætəri] n. 电池
altitude	[ˈæltɪtjuːd] n. 高度；海拔	beginner	[bɪˈgɪnə(r)] n. 初学者
ancestor	[ˈænsestə(r)] n. 祖先	bookshop	[ˈbʊkʃɒp] n. 书店
antenna	[ænˈtenə] n. 天线；触须	brochure	[ˈbrəʊʃə(r)] n. 小册子
antifreeze	[ˈæntifriːz] n. 防冻剂	builder	[ˈbɪldə(r)] n. 建立者
antiseptic	[ˌæntiˈseptɪk] n. 防腐剂, 抗菌剂	button	[ˈbʌtn] n. 按钮
		calculator	[ˈkælkjuleɪtə(r)] n. 计算器
apartment	[əˈpɑːtmənt] n. 公寓	calligraphy	[kəˈlɪgrəfi] n. 书法
apology	[əˈpɒlədʒi] n. 道歉	candle	[ˈkændl] n. 蜡烛
appeal	[əˈpiːl] n. 呼吁；上诉；吸引力	canteen	[kænˈtiːn] n. 食堂
appliance	[əˈplaɪəns] n. 装置	catalogue	[ˈkætəlɒg] n. 目录
applicant	[ˈæplɪkənt] n. 申请人	caterpillar	[ˈkætəpɪlə(r)] n. 毛毛虫
archaeologist	[ˌɑːkiˈɒlədʒɪst] n. 考古学家	cellulose	[ˈseljuləʊs] n. 纤维素
arrival	[əˈraɪvl] n. 到达	cereal	[ˈsɪəriəl] n. 谷物
aspect	[ˈæspekt] n. 方面	champion	[ˈtʃæmpiən] n. 冠军
assurance	[əˈʃʊərəns] n. 保证	chandelier	[ˌʃændəˈlɪə(r)] n. 枝形吊灯
athlete	[ˈæθliːt] n. 运动员	characteristic	[ˌkærəktəˈrɪstɪk] n. 特征
atmosphere	[ˈætməsfɪə(r)] n. 气氛；大气		

childcare	['tʃaɪldkeə(r)] n. 儿童照管	copper	['kɒpə(r)] n. 铜
circle	['sɜːkl] n. 周期；圆	correspondence	[ˌkɒrə'spɒndəns] n. 通信；一致
circulation	[ˌsɜːkjə'leɪʃn] n. 流通；循环	cosmetic	[kɒz'metɪk] n. 化妆品
circumstance	['sɜːkəmstəns] n. 环境；情况	costume	['kɒstjuːm] n. 服装
clinic	['klɪnɪk] n. 诊所	cowboy	['kaʊbɔɪ] n. 牛仔
coastline	['kəʊstlaɪn] n. 海岸线	creature	['kriːtʃə(r)] n. 动物；生物
coconut	['kəʊkənʌt] n. 椰子	critic	['krɪtɪk] n. 批评家，评论家
comedy	['kɒmədi] n. 喜剧	crossbar	['krɒsbɑː(r)] n. 横梁
commission	[kə'mɪʃn] n. 委托；佣金	cuisine	[kwɪ'ziːn] n. 厨房；烹饪
companionship	[kəm'pænjənʃɪp] n. 陪伴	cupboard	['kʌbəd] n. 碗柜
comparison	[kəm'pærɪsn] n. 比较	cushion	['kuʃn] n. 垫子
compensation	[ˌkɒmpen'seɪʃn] n. 补偿；赔偿	cutlery	['kʌtləri] n. 餐具
completion	[kəm'pliːʃn] n. 完成	cycling	['saɪklɪŋ] n. 自行车运动
compressor	[kəm'presə(r)] n. 压缩机；压缩物	daughter	['dɔːtə(r)] n. 女儿
conference	['kɒnfərəns] n. 会议	defence	[dɪ'fens] n. 防御
consultation	[ˌkɒnsl'teɪʃn] n. 咨询	deficiency	[dɪ'fɪʃnsi] n. 缺陷
context	['kɒntekst] n. 环境；上下文	degree	[dɪ'griː] n. 等级；学位
continent	['kɒntɪnənt] n. 大陆，洲	demand	[dɪ'mɑːnd] n. 要求
contrast	['kɒntrɑːst] n. 对比	demonstration	[ˌdemən'streɪʃn] n. 证明
contribution	[ˌkɒntrɪ'bjuːʃn] n. 贡献	destruction	[dɪ'strʌkʃn] n. 破坏
cooker	['kʊkə(r)] n. 炊具	diesel	['diːzl] n. 柴油机；柴油
		digestion	[daɪ'dʒestʃən] n. 消化；理解

disagreement	[ˌdɪsəˈɡriːmənt] *n.* 不一致;不同意
discipline	[ˈdɪsəplɪn] *n.* 学科;纪律
dishwasher	[ˈdɪʃwɒʃə(r)] *n.* 洗碗机
dissatisfaction	[ˌdɪsˌsætɪsˈfækʃn] *n.* 不满意
distinction	[dɪˈstɪŋkʃn] *n.* 区别;特性
distribution	[ˌdɪstrɪˈbjuːʃn] *n.* 分布;分配
district	[ˈdɪstrɪkt] *n.* 区域
diving	[ˈdaɪvɪŋ] *n.* 跳水;潜水
doctor	[ˈdɒktə(r)] *n.* 医生;博士
documentary	[ˌdɒkjuˈmentri] *n.* 纪录片
documentation	[ˌdɒkjumenˈteɪʃn] *n.* 资料,文件
drawer	[drɔː(r)] *n.* 抽屉
drought	[draʊt] *n.* 干旱
dweller	[ˈdwelə(r)] *n.* 居住者
ecologist	[iˈkɒlədʒɪst] *n.* 生态学家
ecology	[iˈkɒlədʒi] *n.* 生态
emperor	[ˈempərə(r)] *n.* 君王
endorsement	[ɪnˈdɔːsmənt] *n.* 认可;背书
engine	[ˈendʒɪn] *n.* 引擎
enquiry	[ɪnˈkwaɪəri] *n.* 询问
enrollment	[ɪnˈrəʊlmənt] *n.* 登记;加入
entitlement	[ɪnˈtaɪtlmənt] *n.* 权利;津贴
erosion	[ɪˈrəʊʒn] *n.* 侵蚀
essence	[ˈesns] *n.* 实质;精华
evaluation	[ɪˌvæljuˈeɪʃn] *n.* 评价;评估
expert	[ˈekspɜːt] *n.* 专家
explanation	[ˌekspləˈneɪʃn] *n.* 解释
export	[ˈekspɔːt] *n.* 出口
extract	[ˈekstrækt] *n.* 摘录
extraction	[ɪkˈstrækʃn] *n.* 取出
eyesight	[ˈaɪsaɪt] *n.* 视力
faculty	[ˈfæklti] *n.* 全体教员
farmland	[ˈfɑːmlænd] *n.* 农田
fashion	[ˈfæʃn] *n.* 时尚
festival	[ˈfestɪvl] *n.* 节日
figure	[ˈfɪɡə(r)] *n.* 数字;人物
filter	[ˈfɪltə(r)] *n.* 过滤器
fireplace	[ˈfaɪəpleɪs] *n.* 壁炉
firework	[ˈfaɪəwɜːk] *n.* 烟火
fisherman	[ˈfɪʃəmən] *n.* 渔夫
flamingo	[fləˈmɪŋɡəʊ] *n.* 火烈鸟
flavour	[ˈfleɪvə(r)] *n.* 香味
flexibility	[ˌfleksəˈbɪləti] *n.* 灵活

flight	[flaɪt] n. 飞行；航班	highway	['haɪweɪ] n. 公路
footprint	['fʊtprɪnt] n. 足迹；脚印	hostel	['hɒstl] n. 旅社，招待所
freedom	['friːdəm] n. 自由	hurricane	['hʌrɪkən] n. 飓风
freshman	['freʃmən] n. 大一学生	hydrogen	['haɪdrədʒən] n. 氢
friction	['frɪkʃn] n. 摩擦	imagination	[ɪˌmædʒɪ'neɪʃn] n. 想象力
funder	['fʌndə(r)] n. 提供资金者	impatience	[ɪm'peɪʃns] n. 不耐烦
future	['fjuːtʃə(r)] n. 未来；期货	inconvenience	[ˌɪnkən'viːniəns] n. 不便
geography	[dʒi'ɒɡrəfi] n. 地理	infant	['ɪnfənt] n. 婴儿
graduation	[ˌɡrædʒu'eɪʃn] n. 毕业	infection	[ɪn'fekʃn] n. 感染
grammar	['ɡræmə(r)] n. 语法	influence	['ɪnfluəns] n. 影响
graphite	['ɡræfaɪt] n. 石墨	ingredient	[ɪn'ɡriːdiənt] n. 要素
greenhouse	['ɡriːnhaʊs] n. 温室	inhabitant	[ɪn'hæbɪtənt] n. 居住者
greeting	['ɡriːtɪŋ] n. 问候	innocence	['ɪnəsns] n. 清白
grouping	['ɡruːpɪŋ] n. 分组	insect	['ɪnsekt] n. 昆虫
growth	[ɡrəʊθ] n. 增长	insecticide	[ɪn'sektɪsaɪd] n. 杀虫剂
habitant	['hæbɪtənt] n. 居住者	instinct	['ɪnstɪŋkt] n. 本能，直觉
habitat	['hæbɪtæt] n. 栖息地	instruction	[ɪn'strʌkʃn] n. 指令；指导
handout	['hændaʊt] n. 课堂讲义	instructor	[ɪn'strʌktə(r)] n. 教师；指导者
harbour	['hɑːbə(r)] n. 港口		
hazard	['hæzəd] n. 危险	insulation	[ˌɪnsju'leɪʃn] n. 绝缘；隔离
heading	['hedɪŋ] n. 标题	intelligence	[ɪn'telɪdʒəns] n. 智力
hibernation	[ˌhaɪbə'neɪʃn] n. 冬眠	interest	['ɪntrəst] n. 兴趣；利益

interference	[ˌɪntəˈfɪərəns] n. 干扰；干涉	mainland	[ˈmeɪnlənd] n. 大陆；本土
interruption	[ˌɪntəˈrʌpʃn] n. 中断；干扰	management	[ˈmænɪdʒmənt] n. 管理
intrigue	[ɪnˈtriːg] n. 阴谋	manufacturer	[ˌmænjuˈfæktʃərə(r)] n. 制造商
invasion	[ɪnˈveɪʒn] n. 入侵	marriage	[ˈmærɪdʒ] n. 婚姻
invoice	[ˈɪnvɔɪs] n. 发票	masonry	[ˈmeɪsənri] n. 石工
jacket	[ˈdʒækɪt] n. 短上衣；夹克	masterpiece	[ˈmɑːstəpiːs] n. 杰作
jewellery	[ˈdʒuːəlri] n. 珠宝	mastery	[ˈmɑːstəri] n. 掌握；精通
journal	[ˈdʒɜːnl] n. 杂志	medicine	[ˈmedsn] n. 药；医学
journalism	[ˈdʒɜːnəlɪzəm] n. 新闻业	mentor	[ˈmentɔː(r)] n. 导师
journey	[ˈdʒɜːni] n. 旅行	metallurgy	[məˈtælədʒi] n. 冶金
laboratory	[ləˈbɒrətri] n. 实验室	meteorology	[ˌmiːtiəˈrɒlədʒi] n. 气象学
landlord	[ˈlændlɔːd] n. 房东	microscope	[ˈmaɪkrəskəʊp] n. 显微镜
laundry	[ˈlɔːndri] n. 洗衣房	million	[ˈmɪljən] n. 百万
lawyer	[ˈlɔɪə(r)] n. 律师	minimum	[ˈmɪnɪməm] n. 最小值
leadership	[ˈliːdəʃɪp] n. 领导能力	minority	[maɪˈnɒrəti] n. 少数民族；少数派
length	[leŋθ] n. 长度	module	[ˈmɒdjuːl] n. 模块
librarian	[laɪˈbreəriən] n. 图书管理员	moisture	[ˈmɔɪstʃə(r)] n. 水分；潮湿
livestock	[ˈlaɪvstɒk] n. 牲畜	monarch	[ˈmɒnək] n. 君主，帝王
luxury	[ˈlʌkʃəri] n. 奢侈；奢侈品	motivation	[ˌməʊtɪˈveɪʃn] n. 动机
machine	[məˈʃiːn] n. 机器	musician	[mjuˈzɪʃn] n. 音乐家
magazine	[ˌmægəˈziːn] n. 杂志	napkin	[ˈnæpkɪn] n. 餐巾纸
magnet	[ˈmægnət] n. 磁铁		

newsletter	['nju:zletə(r)] *n.* 内部通讯	platform	['plætfɔ:m] *n.* 平台；站台
nightlife	['naɪtlaɪf] *n.* 夜生活	platinum	['plætɪnəm] *n.* 铂
notebook	['nəʊtbʊk] *n.* 笔记本	pocket	['pɒkɪt] *n.* 口袋
noticeboard	['nəʊtɪsbɔ:d] *n.* 布告栏	politician	[,pɒlə'tɪʃn] *n.* 政治家
object	['ɒbdʒɪkt] *n.* 物体	pollen	['pɒlən] *n.* 花粉
objectivity	[,ɒbdʒek'tɪvəti] *n.* 客观	portfolio	[pɔ:t'fəʊliəʊ] *n.* 公文包；文件夹
opinion	[ə'pɪnjən] *n.* 意见		
opportunity	[,ɒpə'tju:nəti] *n.* 机会	poster	['pəʊstə(r)] *n.* 海报
opposition	[,ɒpə'zɪʃn] *n.* 反对	preference	['prefrəns] *n.* 偏好
organiser	['ɔ:gənaɪzə(r)] *n.* 组织者	president	['prezɪdənt] *n.* 董事长；校长
originality	[ə,rɪdʒə'næləti] *n.* 创意；独创性	pressure	['preʃə(r)] *n.* 压力
		principle	['prɪnsəpl] *n.* 原则
outbreak	['aʊtbreɪk] *n.* 爆发	printing	['prɪntɪŋ] *n.* 印刷
outcome	['aʊtkʌm] *n.* 结果；成果	procedure	[prə'si:dʒə(r)] *n.* 程序；步骤
oyster	['ɔɪstə(r)] *n.* 牡蛎	proficiency	[prə'fɪʃnsi] *n.* 熟练
palace	['pæləs] *n.* 宫殿	profit	['prɒfɪt] *n.* 利润；利益
passenger	['pæsɪndʒə(r)] *n.* 旅客；乘客	property	['prɒpəti] *n.* 性质；财产
passion	['pæʃn] *n.* 激情，热情	publishing	['pʌblɪʃɪŋ] *n.* 出版；出版业
patient	['peɪʃnt] *n.* 病人	punctuality	[,pʌŋktʃu'æləti] *n.* 守时
penalty	['penəlti] *n.* 罚款；处罚	pyramid	['pɪrəmɪd] *n.* 金字塔
permission	[pə'mɪʃn] *n.* 允许，许可	realism	['ri:əlɪzəm] *n.* 现实主义
photocopy	['fəʊtəʊkɒpi] *n.* 复印	receiver	[rɪ'si:və(r)] *n.* 接收者；接收器
photography	[fə'tɒɡrəfi] *n.* 摄影	recession	[rɪ'seʃn] *n.* 衰退

reconstruction	[ˌriːkənˈstrʌkʃn] n. 重建	sector	[ˈsektə(r)] n. 部门
refrigerator	[rɪˈfrɪdʒəreɪtə(r)] n. 冰箱，冷藏库	seminar	[ˈsemɪnɑː(r)] n. 讨论会
rehearsal	[rɪˈhɜːsl] n. 排练；预演	setting	[ˈsetɪŋ] n. 环境；安装
relaxation	[ˌriːlækˈseɪʃn] n. 放松	shortage	[ˈʃɔːtɪdʒ] n. 缺乏
reliance	[rɪˈlaɪəns] n. 依赖	sightseeing	[ˈsaɪtsiːɪŋ] n. 观光
relocation	[ˌriːləʊˈkeɪʃn] n. 重新安置	simulation	[ˌsɪmjuˈleɪʃn] n. 模拟；模仿
reminder	[rɪˈmaɪndə(r)] n. 提示	situation	[ˌsɪtʃuˈeɪʃn] n. 情况；形势
resident	[ˈrezɪdənt] n. 居民	skeleton	[ˈskelɪtn] n. 骨架
revision	[rɪˈvɪʒn] n. 修改	sliver	[ˈslɪvə(r)] n. 梳毛；裂片
rhythm	[ˈrɪðəm] n. 节奏	soldier	[ˈsəʊldʒə(r)] n. 军人
ritual	[ˈrɪtʃuəl] n. 仪式	solution	[səˈluːʃn] n. 解决方案；溶液
routine	[ruːˈtiːn] n. 惯例	soybean	[ˈsɔɪbiːn] n. 大豆；黄豆
rumour	[ˈruːmə(r)] n. 谣言	specialist	[ˈspeʃəlɪst] n. 专家
saliva	[səˈlaɪvə] n. 唾液	speciality	[ˌspeʃiˈæləti] n. 专业；特性
sanctuary	[ˈsæŋktʃuəri] n. 避难所	spelling	[ˈspelɪŋ] n. 拼写
scenario	[səˈnɑːriəʊ] n. 场景	spider	[ˈspaɪdə(r)] n. 蜘蛛
scholarship	[ˈskɒləʃɪp] n. 奖学金	spirit	[ˈspɪrɪt] n. 精神；心灵
scientist	[ˈsaɪəntɪst] n. 科学家	sponge	[spʌndʒ] n. 海绵
script	[skrɪpt] n. 剧本	sponsorship	[ˈspɒnsəʃɪp] n. 赞助；发起
seabed	[ˈsiːbed] n. 海底，海床	spread	[spred] n. 传播；延伸
seaside	[ˈsiːsaɪd] n. 海边	sprinter	[ˈsprɪntə(r)] n. 短跑选手
section	[ˈsekʃn] n. 部分；部门	stairway	[ˈsteəweɪ] n. 楼梯

standpoint	['stændpɔɪnt] n. 立场；观点	technologist	[tek'nɒlədʒɪst] n. 技术专家
starch	[staːtʃ] n. 淀粉	telecommunication	[ˌtelikəˌmjuːnɪ'keɪʃn] n. 远程通信
starvation	[staː'veɪʃn] n. 饥饿	temple	['templ] n. 寺庙
statement	['steɪtmənt] n. 陈述	tenant	['tenənt] n. 房客
statue	['stætʃuː] n. 雕像	terrace	['terəs] n. 露天平台；梯田
storeroom	['stɔːrʊm] n. 库房	textbook	['tekstbʊk] n. 课本
storyline	['stɔːrilaɪn] n. 故事情节	texture	['tekstʃə(r)] n. 纹理
stream	[striːm] n. 溪流	thermostat	['θɜːməstæt] n. 恒温器
structure	['strʌktʃə(r)] n. 结构	timber	['tɪmbə(r)] n. 木材
subliminal	[ˌsʌb'lɪmɪnl] n. 潜意识	tortoise	['tɔːtəs] n. 乌龟
subsidiary	[səb'sɪdiəri] n. 子公司；辅助者	transaction	[træn'zækʃn] n. 交易
substance	['sʌbstəns] n. 物质；实质	transcription	[træn'skrɪpʃn] n. 抄写
subtitle	['sʌbtaɪtl] n. 副标题	transition	[træn'zɪʃn] n. 过渡
supply	[sə'plaɪ] n. 供给	translation	[trænz'leɪʃn] n. 翻译
surface	['sɜːfɪs] n. 表面	treasure	['treʒə(r)] n. 财富
surfing	['sɜːfɪŋ] n. 冲浪	trumpet	['trʌmpɪt] n. 喇叭
switch	[swɪtʃ] n. 开关；转变	turbine	['tɜːbaɪn] n. 涡轮机
symbol	['sɪmbl] n. 象征；符号	tutorial	[tjuː'tɔːriəl] n. 辅导课
tablet	['tæblət] n. 药片；平板电脑	umbrella	[ʌm'brelə] n. 雨伞
takeaway	['teɪkəweɪ] n. 外卖	undergraduate	[ˌʌndə'grædʒuət] n. 本科生
takeover	['teɪkəʊvə(r)] n. 接管	underneath	[ˌʌndə'niːθ] n. 底部
tanker	['tæŋkə(r)] n. 油轮	update	[ˌʌp'deɪt] n. 更新

utensil	[juːˈtensl] *n.* 用具，器皿	viewpoint	[ˈvjuːpɔɪnt] *n.* 观点；视角
vacuum	[ˈvækjuːm] *n.* 真空；空缺	visibility	[ˌvɪzəˈbɪləti] *n.* 能见度
valley	[ˈvæli] *n.* 山谷	wallpaper	[ˈwɔːlpeɪpə(r)] *n.* 墙纸
variation	[ˌveəriˈeɪʃn] *n.* 变化；变异	weapon	[ˈwepən] *n.* 武器
vegetable	[ˈvedʒtəbl] *n.* 蔬菜	weekend	[ˌwiːkˈend] *n.* 周末
ventilator	[ˈventɪleɪtə(r)] *n.* 通风设备	wetland	[ˈwetlənd] *n.* 湿地；沼泽
version	[ˈvɜːʃn] *n.* 版本	wheelchair	[ˈwiːltʃeə(r)] *n.* 轮椅
vetting	[ˈvetɪŋ] *n.* 审查；审核	windsurfing	[ˈwɪndsɜːfɪŋ] *n.* 帆板
vibration	[vaɪˈbreɪʃn] *n.* 振动	workload	[ˈwɜːkləʊd] *n.* 工作量
victim	[ˈvɪktɪm] *n.* 受害人	workplace	[ˈwɜːkpleɪs] *n.* 工作场所

二 复数名词

children	[ˈtʃɪldrən] *n.* 儿童	prices	[ˈpraɪsɪz] *n.* 价格
parents	[ˈpeərənts] *n.* 父母	resources	[rɪˈsɔːsɪz] *n.* 资源
photographs	[ˈfəʊtəɡrɑːfs] *n.* 照片	companies	[ˈkʌmpəniz] *n.* 公司
months	[mʌnθs] *n.* 月份	factories	[ˈfæktəriz] *n.* 工厂
activities	[ækˈtɪvətiz] *n.* 活动	guests	[ɡests] *n.* 客人
courses	[ˈkɔːsɪz] *n.* 课程	holes	[həʊlz] *n.* 洞
tools	[tuːlz] *n.* 工具	memories	[ˈmeməriz] *n.* 记忆
adults	[ˈædʌlts] *n.* 成年人	parties	[ˈpɑːtiz] *n.* 聚会
classes	[ˈklɑːsɪz] *n.* 班级	photos	[ˈfəʊtəʊz] *n.* 照片
facilities	[fəˈsɪlətiz] *n.* 设施	profits	[ˈprɒfɪts] *n.* 利润

rats	[ræts] n. 老鼠	bushes	[bʊʃɪz] n. 灌木丛
stones	[stəʊnz] n. 石头	categories	['kætəgəriz] n. 种类，分类
bones	[bəʊnz] n. 骨骼	changes	['tʃeɪndʒɪz] n. 变化
caves	[keɪvz] n. 洞穴	chicks	[tʃɪks] n. 小鸡
feathers	['feðəz] n. 羽毛	cities	['sɪtɪz] n. 城市
fees	[fiːz] n. 费用	clients	['klaɪənts] n. 客户
humans	['hjuːmənz] n. 人类	clothes	[kləʊðz] n. 衣服
minerals	['mɪnərəlz] n. 矿物	congratulations	[kən,grætʃə'leɪʃnz] n. 祝贺
movies	['muːviz] n. 电影	cords	[kɔːdz] n. 绳索
relatives	['relətɪvz] n. 亲戚	experiences	[ɪk'spɪəriənsɪz] n. 经历
rocks	[rɒks] n. 岩石	files	[faɪlz] n. 文件夹
seeds	[siːdz] n. 种子	frogs	[frɒgz] n. 青蛙
strategies	['strætədʒiz] n. 策略	furs	[fɜːz] n. 毛皮
tastes	[teɪsts] n. 口味	grades	[greɪdz] n. 分数
automobiles	['ɔːtəməbiːlz] n. 汽车	headlines	['hedlaɪnz] n. 标题
babies	['beɪbiz] n. 婴儿	holidays	['hɒlədeɪz] n. 假日
bacteria	[bæk'tɪəriə] n. 细菌	labels	['leɪblz] n. 标签
biscuits	['bɪskɪts] n. 饼干	meals	[miːlz] n. 餐
boards	[bɔːdz] n. 董事会	methods	['meθədz] n. 方法
booths	[buːðz] n. 展台；电话亭	mirrors	['mɪrəz] n. 镜子
boots	[buːts] n. 靴子	notes	[nəʊts] n. 笔记
bricks	[brɪks] n. 砖	obstacles	['ɒbstəklz] n. 障碍

offers	['ɒfəz] n. 提议；出价	accents	['æksənts] n. 口音
pilots	['paɪləts] n. 飞行员	accountants	[ə'kaʊntənts] n. 会计人员
planets	['plænɪts] n. 行星	accounts	[ə'kaʊnts] n. 账户
plates	[pleɪts] n. 盘子	aggressions	[ə'greʃnz] n. 侵略
players	['pleɪəz] n. 球员	aims	[aims] n. 目的
pots	[pɒts] n. 壶	airlines	['eəlaɪnz] n. 航空公司
professionals	[prə'feʃənlz] n. 专业人士	allergies	['ælədʒiz] n. 过敏
residents	['rezɪdənts] n. 居民	angles	['æŋglz] n. 角度
ropes	[rəʊps] n. 绳索	antiques	[æn'tiːks] n. 古董
seagulls	['siːgʌlz] n. 海鸥	arguments	['ɑːgjumənts] n. 论据
species	['spiːʃiːz] n. 物种	arrows	['ærəʊz] n. 箭
staircases	['steəkeɪsɪz] n. 楼梯	articles	['ɑːtɪklz] n. 文章
stitches	['stɪtʃɪz] n. 缝线	awards	[ə'wɔːdz] n. 奖品
techniques	[tek'niːks] n. 技巧	badges	[bædʒɪz] n. 徽章
teenagers	['tiːneɪdʒəz] n. 青少年	barriers	['bæriəz] n. 障碍
theories	['θɪəriz] n. 理论	basins	['beɪsnz] n. 盆地
tickets	['tɪkɪts] n. 票	bats	[bæts] n. 蝙蝠
towels	['taʊəlz] n. 毛巾	behaviours	[bɪ'heɪvjəz] n. 行为
visuals	['vɪʒuəlz] n. 视觉效果	bins	[bɪnz] n. 箱子
wages	['weɪdʒɪz] n. 工资	biologists	[baɪ'ɒlədʒɪsts] n. 生物学家
whales	[weɪlz] n. 鲸	blocks	[blɒks] n. 阻碍
aboriginals	[ˌæbə'rɪdʒənlz] n. 土著人	boilers	['bɔɪləz] n. 锅炉

boxes	['bɒksɪz] n. 盒	crops	[krɒps] n. 作物
branches	['brɑːntʃɪz] n. 分支机构	diaries	['daɪəriz] n. 日记
brushes	['brʌʃɪz] n. 刷子	differences	['dɪfrənsɪz] n. 分歧
bulbs	[bʌlbz] n. 灯泡	difficulties	['dɪfɪkəltiz] n. 困难
butterflies	['bʌtəflaɪz] n. 蝴蝶	dolls	[dɒlz] n. 玩偶
causes	['kɔːzɪz] n. 原因	dolphins	['dɒlfɪnz] n. 海豚
charities	['tʃærətiz] n. 慈善机构	drinks	[drɪŋks] n. 饮料
claws	[klɔːz] n. 爪	elements	['elɪmənts] n. 元素
clips	[klɪps] n. 片段	errors	['erəz] n. 错误
clubs	[klʌbz] n. 俱乐部	events	[ɪ'vents] n. 事件
coats	[kəʊts] n. 外套	exams	[ɪg'zæms] n. 考试
collectors	[kə'lektəz] n. 收藏家	excavations	[ˌekskə'veɪʃnz] n. 挖掘
competitors	[kəm'petɪtəz] n. 竞争对手	exercises	['eksəsaɪzɪz] n. 练习
complaints	[kəm'pleɪnts] n. 抱怨	expenses	[ɪk'spensɪz] n. 费用
components	[kəm'pəʊnənts] n. 组件	extinguishers	[ɪk'stɪŋgwɪʃəz] n. 灭火器
connectives	[kə'nektɪvz] n. 连接词	feelings	['fiːlɪŋz] n. 感情
corners	['kɔːnəz] n. 角落	films	[fɪlmz] n. 电影
corridors	['kɒrɪdɔːz] n. 走廊	fluids	['fluːɪdz] n. 流体
counterparts	['kaʊntəpɑːts] n. 对应的人或物	forms	[fɔːmz] n. 形式
countries	['kʌntriz] n. 国家	fossils	['fɒslz] n. 化石
crimes	[kraɪmz] n. 犯罪	frames	[freɪmz] n. 框架
criteria	[kraɪ'tɪəriə] n. 标准	fruits	[fruːts] n. 果实

fuels	['fju:əlz] n. 燃料	items	['aɪtəmz] n. 项目
galleries	['gælərɪz] n. 美术馆	knives	[naɪvz] n. 刀具
gardens	['gɑ:dnz] n. 花园	laboratories	[lə'bɒrətriz] n. 实验室
gases	['gæsɪz] n. 气体	ladybugs	['leɪdibʌgz] n. 瓢虫
genes	[dʒi:nz] n. 基因	landmarks	['lændmɑ:ks] n. 地标
glaciers	[glacierz] n. 冰川	languages	['læŋgwɪdʒɪz] n. 语言
glasses	['glɑ:sɪz] n. 玻璃杯	laptops	['læptɒps] n. 笔记本电脑
gloves	[glʌvz] n. 手套	layers	['leɪəz] n. 层
guidelines	['gaɪdlaɪnz] n. 指导方针	leaves	[li:vz] n. 树叶
habits	['hæbɪts] n. 习惯	limitations	[ˌlɪmɪ'teɪʃnz] n. 局限性
hampers	['hæmpəz] n. 带盖的大篮子	links	[lɪŋks] n. 链接
helpers	['helpəz] n. 助手	lizards	['lɪzədz] n. 蜥蜴
hormones	['hɔ:məunz] n. 激素	locals	['ləuklz] n. 当地人
horses	['hɔ:sɪz] n. 马	machines	[mə'ʃi:nz] n. 机器
hotels	[həu'telz] n. 酒店; 旅馆	majors	['meɪdʒəz] n. 专业
houses	['hauzɪz] n. 房屋	mammals	['mæmlz] n. 哺乳动物
huts	[hʌts] n. 小屋	merchants	['mɜ:tʃənts] n. 商人
industries	['ɪndəstrɪz] n. 行业	mites	[maɪts] n. 螨虫
injuries	['ɪndʒərɪz] n. 伤害	monsters	['mɒnstəz] n. 怪兽
institutions	[ˌɪnstɪ'tju:ʃnz] n. 机构	monuments	['mɒnjuments] n. 纪念碑
intermediaries	[ˌɪntə'mi:diəriz] n. 中间商	motorbikes	['məutəbaɪks] n. 摩托车
issues	['ɪʃu:z] n. 问题	musicians	[mju'zɪʃnz] n. 音乐家

nationalities	[ˌnæʃəˈnælətiz] n. 国籍		salads	[ˈsælədz] n. 沙拉
negotiations	[nɪˌɡəʊʃiˈeɪʃnz] n. 谈判		samples	[ˈsɑːmplz] n. 样品
nets	[nets] n. 网		seals	[siːlz] n. 海豹
outlets	[ˈaʊtlets] n. 经销店		services	[ˈsɜːvɪsɪz] n. 服务
peers	[pɪəz] n. 同龄人		settlers	[ˈsetləz] n. 定居者
penknives	[ˈpennaɪvz] n. 铅笔刀		shells	[ʃelz] n. 贝壳
pipes	[paɪps] n. 管		signposts	[ˈsaɪnpəʊsts] n. 路标
pirates	[ˈpaɪrəts] n. 海盗		silverwares	[ˈsɪlvəweəz] n. 银器
planes	[pleɪnz] n. 飞机		sizes	[ˈsaɪzɪz] n. 尺寸
plots	[plɒts] n. 阴谋		snacks	[snæks] n. 小吃
postcards	[ˈpəʊstkɑːdz] n. 明信片		socks	[sɒks] n. 袜子
potatoes	[pəˈteɪtəʊz] n. 土豆		sources	[ˈsɔːsɪz] n. 来源
prints	[prɪnts] n. 印刷品		squirrels	[ˈskwɪrəlz] n. 松鼠
purposes	[ˈpɜːpəsɪz] n. 目的		stages	[ˈsteɪdʒɪz] n. 舞台
recordings	[rɪˈkɔːdɪŋz] n. 录音		stairs	[steəz] n. 楼梯
repairs	[rɪˈpeəz] n. 修理工作		steamships	[ˈstiːmʃɪps] n. 轮船
responsibilities	[rɪˌspɒnsəˈbɪlətiz] n. 责任		stickers	[ˈstɪkəz] n. 贴纸
restorers	[rɪˈstɔːrəz] n. 修复者		stores	[stɔːz] n. 商店
riders	[ˈraɪdəz] n. 骑手		stories	[ˈstɔːriz] n. 故事
rivals	[ˈraɪvlz] n. 对手		strips	[strɪps] n. 条状物
robots	[ˈrəʊbɒts] n. 机器人		sunglasses	[ˈsʌnglɑːsɪz] n. 太阳镜
sailors	[ˈseɪləz] n. 水手		swans	[swɒnz] n. 天鹅

talks	[tɔːks] *n.* 谈话	tricks	[trɪks] *n.* 诡计
tanks	[tanks] *n.* 坦克	trips	[trɪps] *n.* 旅行
tasks	[tɑːsks] *n.* 任务	vacancies	['veɪkənsɪz] *n.* 空缺
taxes	['tæksɪz] *n.* 税	varieties	[və'raɪətɪz] *n.* 种类
texts	[teksts] *n.* 文本	views	[vjuːz] *n.* 意见
tips	[tɪps] *n.* 提示	villagers	['vɪlɪdʒəz] *n.* 村民
towers	['taʊəz] *n.* 塔	weeds	[wiːdz] *n.* 杂草
toys	[tɔɪz] *n.* 玩具	wheels	[wiːlz] *n.* 车轮
tracks	[træks] *n.* 轨道	wounds	[wuːndz] *n.* 伤口
trails	[treɪlz] *n.* 踪迹	zones	[zəʊnz] *n.* 地带

三 动词

interview	['ɪntəvjuː] *v.* 采访；面试	produce	[prə'djuːs] *v.* 生产；引起
collect	[kə'lekt] *v.* 收集	provide	[prə'vaɪd] *v.* 提供
accept	[ək'sept] *v.* 接受	register	['redʒɪstə(r)] *v.* 登记；注册
attend	[ə'tend] *v.* 出席	achieve	[ə'tʃiːv] *v.* 获得
cause	[kɔːz] *v.* 引起	decrease	[dɪ'kriːs] *v.* 减少
include	[ɪn'kluːd] *v.* 包括	degrade	[dɪ'greɪd] *v.* 降低
recruit	[rɪ'kruːt] *v.* 征招	dismiss	[dɪs'mɪs] *v.* 解散；解雇
decline	[dɪ'klaɪn] *v.* 下降；衰落	distinguish	[dɪ'stɪŋgwɪʃ] *v.* 辨别
encourage	[ɪn'kʌrɪdʒ] *v.* 鼓励	expand	[ɪk'spænd] *v.* 发展
exchange	[ɪks'tʃeɪndʒ] *v.* 交换	impose	[ɪm'pəʊz] *v.* 强加于；征税

improve	[ɪm'pruːv] v. 改善；提高	deploy	[dɪ'plɔɪ] v. 展开
perform	[pə'fɔːm] v. 执行	destroy	[dɪ'strɔɪ] v. 破坏
prefer	[prɪ'fɜː(r)] v. 更喜欢	enlarge	[ɪn'lɑːdʒ] v. 扩大；放大
preserve	[prɪ'zɜːv] v. 保存	evaluate	[ɪ'væljueɪt] v. 评价
recommend	[ˌrekə'mend] v. 推荐	highlight	['haɪlaɪt] v. 强调
reject	[rɪ'dʒekt] v. 拒绝	identify	[aɪ'dentɪfaɪ] v. 确定；识别
reserve	[rɪ'zɜːv] v. 预订；保留	ignore	[ɪg'nɔː(r)] v. 忽视
restrict	[rɪ'strɪkt] v. 限制	indicate	['ɪndɪkeɪt] v. 表明
store	[stɔː(r)] v. 储存	inspire	[ɪn'spaɪə(r)] v. 激发
surprise	[sə'praɪz] v. 使吃惊	involve	[ɪn'vɒlv] v. 包含
absorb	[əb'zɔːb] v. 吸收；理解	launch	[lɔːntʃ] v. 发射；发起
acquire	[ə'kwaɪə(r)] v. 获得	measure	['meʒə(r)] v. 测量
advertise	['ædvətaɪz] v. 做广告	occur	[ə'kɜː(r)] v. 发生
advise	[əd'vaɪz] v. 建议	persuade	[pə'sweɪd] v. 说服
allow	[ə'laʊ] v. 允许	polish	['pɒlɪʃ] v. 打磨
appear	[ə'pɪə(r)] v. 出现；显得	pose	[pəʊz] v. 提出；造成
apply	[ə'plaɪ] v. 申请；应用	predict	[prɪ'dɪkt] v. 预测
appreciate	[ə'priːʃieɪt] v. 欣赏；感激	prepare	[prɪ'peə(r)] v. 准备
celebrate	['selɪbreɪt] v. 庆祝	purchase	['pɜːtʃəs] v. 购买
compare	[kəm'peə(r)] v. 比较	quarrel	['kwɒrəl] v. 吵架
conduct	[kən'dʌkt] v. 实施；引导	raise	[reɪz] v. 提高；筹集；养育
convert	[kən'vɜːt] v. 转换	range	[reɪndʒ] v. 变动

refer	[rɪˈfɜː(r)] v. 参考; 提到	attack	[əˈtæk] v. 攻击
reflect	[rɪˈflekt] v. 反映; 反思	attract	[əˈtrækt] v. 吸引
replace	[rɪˈpleɪs] v. 代替	bargain	[ˈbɑːɡən] v. 讨价还价
resent	[rɪˈzent] v. 怨恨	bounce	[baʊns] v. 弹起
reveal	[rɪˈviːl] v. 揭示	calculate	[ˈkælkjuleɪt] v. 计算
simplify	[ˈsɪmplɪfaɪ] v. 简化	capture	[ˈkæptʃə(r)] v. 俘获
ski	[skiː] v. 滑雪	carve	[kɑːv] v. 雕刻
sneeze	[sniːz] v. 打喷嚏	cater	[ˈkeɪtə(r)] v. 迎合
specialize	[ˈspeʃəlaɪz] v. 专门从事	claim	[kleɪm] v. 宣称
stick	[stɪk] v. 刺, 戳	classify	[ˈklæsɪfaɪ] v. 分类
survive	[səˈvaɪv] v. 幸存	combine	[kəmˈbaɪn] v. 结合
transmit	[trænzˈmɪt] v. 传输	commemorate	[kəˈmeməreɪt] v. 纪念
witness	[ˈwɪtnəs] v. 见证	compensate	[ˈkɒmpenseɪt] v. 补偿
acknowledge	[əkˈnɒlɪdʒ] v. 承认	compete	[kəmˈpiːt] v. 竞争; 比赛
activate	[ˈæktɪveɪt] v. 激活	complain	[kəmˈpleɪn] v. 投诉; 抱怨
adjust	[əˈdʒʌst] v. 调整, 使适合	complete	[kəmˈpliːt] v. 完成
affect	[əˈfekt] v. 影响; 感动	compost	[ˈkɒmpɒst] v. 施堆肥
appoint	[əˈpɔɪnt] v. 任命; 指定	concentrate	[ˈkɒnsntreɪt] v. 集中
arrange	[əˈreɪndʒ] v. 安排; 排列	concern	[kənˈsɜːn] v. 关心
assist	[əˈsɪst] v. 帮助	construct	[kənˈstrʌkt] v. 建造
assume	[əˈsjuːm] v. 假设	consult	[kənˈsʌlt] v. 咨询
attach	[əˈtætʃ] v. 附加	contain	[kənˈteɪn] v. 包含

contribute	[kən'trɪbjuːt] v. 贡献	express	[ɪk'spres] v. 表达
convince	[kən'vɪns] v. 使信服	grant	[graːnt] v. 授予
cultivate	['kʌltɪveɪt] v. 培养	harden	['haːdn] v. 变硬
decompose	[ˌdiːkəm'pəʊz] v. 分解	hibernate	['haɪbəneɪt] v. 冬眠
demonstrate	['demənstreɪt] v. 证明	import	['ɪmpɔːt] v. 进口
derive	[dɪ'raɪv] v. 源于	increase	[ɪn'kriːs] v. 增加
describe	[dɪ'skraɪb] v. 描述	inhabit	[ɪn'hæbɪt] v. 居住于
detect	[dɪ'tekt] v. 察觉；探测	inspect	[ɪn'spekt] v. 检查
discover	[dɪ'skʌvə(r)] v. 发现	install	[ɪn'stɔːl] v. 安装
donate	[dəʊ'neɪt] v. 捐赠	invade	[ɪn'veɪd] v. 侵略
doubt	[daʊt] v. 怀疑	investigate	[ɪn'vestɪgeɪt] v. 调查
enhance	[ɪn'haːns] v. 提高；加强	manage	['mænɪdʒ] v. 管理
enrol	[ɪn'rəʊl] v. 招收	migrate	[maɪ'greɪt] v. 移居
ensure	[ɪn'ʃʊə(r)] v. 确保	minimize	['mɪnɪmaɪz] v. 最小化
evaporate	[ɪ'væpəreɪt] v. 蒸发	miscalculate	[ˌmɪs'kælkjuleɪt] v. 误算
exaggerate	[ɪg'zædʒəreɪt] v. 扩大	misunderstand	[ˌmɪsʌndə'stænd] v. 误解
exclude	[ɪk'skluːd] v. 排除	observe	[əb'zɜːv] v. 观察；遵循
exist	[ɪg'zɪst] v. 存在	obtain	[əb'teɪn] v. 获得
explain	[ɪk'spleɪn] v. 解释	occupy	['ɒkjupaɪ] v. 占据
explode	[ɪk'spləʊd] v. 爆炸	operate	['ɒpəreɪt] v. 操作
explore	[ɪk'splɔː(r)] v. 探索	order	['ɔːdə(r)] v. 命令；订购
expose	[ɪk'spəʊz] v. 暴露	organize	['ɔːgənaɪz] v. 组织

originate	[əˈrɪdʒɪneɪt] v. 发源于	require	[rɪˈkwaɪə(r)] v. 要求
overcome	[ˌəʊvəˈkʌm] v. 克服	resemble	[rɪˈzembl] v. 类似，像
overestimate	[ˌəʊvərˈestɪmeɪt] v. 高估	retrain	[ˌriːˈtreɪn] v. 再教育；再训练
overlook	[ˌəʊvəˈlʊk] v. 忽略	sense	[sens] v. 感觉到
oversee	[ˌəʊvəˈsiː] v. 监督	shoot	[ʃuːt] v. 射击
participate	[pɑːˈtɪsɪpeɪt] v. 参与	snail	[sneɪl] v. 缓慢移动
praise	[preɪz] v. 赞扬	socialize	[ˈsəʊʃəlaɪz] v. 社交
prohibit	[prəˈhɪbɪt] v. 禁止	squash	[skwɒʃ] v. 挤压
promote	[prəˈməʊt] v. 促进；推广	submit	[səbˈmɪt] v. 提交
react	[riˈækt] v. 反应	suggest	[səˈdʒest] v. 提议；暗示
rebuild	[ˌriːˈbɪld] v. 重建	swing	[swɪŋ] v. 摇摆
receive	[rɪˈsiːv] v. 收到；接待	trace	[treɪs] v. 追溯
recognise	[ˈrekəgnaɪz] v. 承认	underline	[ˌʌndəˈlaɪn] v. 强调；在下面画线
recycle	[ˌriːˈsaɪkl] v. 回收；循环		
release	[rɪˈliːs] v. 释放	varnish	[ˈvɑːnɪʃ] v. 装饰
represent	[ˌreprɪˈzent] v. 代表	withhold	[wɪðˈhəʊld] v. 保留

四 形容词

plastic	[ˈplæstɪk] adj. 塑料的	additional	[əˈdɪʃənl] adj. 附加的；额外的
negative	[ˈnegətɪv] adj. 消极的		
special	[ˈspeʃl] adj. 特别的	extinct	[ɪkˈstɪŋkt] adj. 灭绝的
		main	[meɪn] adj. 主要的

convenient	[kən'viːniənt] *adj.* 方便的

practical ['præktɪkl] *adj.* 实际的

different ['dɪfrənt] *adj.* 不同的

relevant ['reləvənt] *adj.* 相关的

social ['səʊʃl] *adj.* 社会的；社交的

various ['veəriəs] *adj.* 各种各样的

available [ə'veɪləbl] *adj.* 可使用的

chemical ['kemɪkl] *adj.* 化学的

complex ['kɒmpleks] *adj.* 复杂的

current ['kʌrənt] *adj.* 现在的

dark [dɑːk] *adj.* 黑暗的

flexible ['fleksəbl] *adj.* 灵活的

insufficient [ˌɪnsə'fɪʃnt] *adj.* 不足的

acid ['æsɪd] *adj.* 酸的

commercial [kə'mɜːʃl] *adj.* 商业的

correct [kə'rekt] *adj.* 正确的

electronic [ɪˌlek'trɒnɪk] *adj.* 电子的

enthusiastic [ɪnˌθjuːzi'æstɪk] *adj.* 热情的

external [ɪk'stɜːnl] *adj.* 外部的；表面的

extra ['ekstrə] *adj.* 额外的

fake [feɪk] *adj.* 假的

general ['dʒenrəl] *adj.* 一般的，普通的

genetic [dʒə'netɪk] *adj.* 遗传的；基因的

historical [hɪ'stɒrɪkl] *adj.* 历史的

important [ɪm'pɔːtnt] *adj.* 重要的

inaccurate [ɪn'ækjərət] *adj.* 不准确的

inadequate [ɪn'ædɪkwət] *adj.* 不充分的

intermediate [ˌɪntə'miːdiət] *adj.* 中间的

international [ˌɪntə'næʃnəl] *adj.* 国际的

legal ['liːgl] *adj.* 法律的；合法的

necessary ['nesəsəri] *adj.* 必要的

original [ə'rɪdʒənl] *adj.* 最初的

personal ['pɜːsənl] *adj.* 个人的

popular ['pɒpjələ(r)] *adj.* 流行的

previous ['priːviəs] *adj.* 以前的

psychological [ˌsaɪkə'lɒdʒɪkl] *adj.* 心理的

reliable [rɪ'laɪəbl] *adj.* 可靠的

retail ['riːteɪl] *adj.* 零售的

seasonal ['siːzənl] *adj.* 季节的；周期性的

similar ['sɪmələ(r)] *adj.* 相似的

suitable ['suːtəbl] *adj.* 合适的

theoretical	[ˌθɪə'retɪkl] *adj.* 理论上的
unusual	[ʌn'juːʒuəl] *adj.* 不寻常的
valuable	['væljuəbl] *adj.* 有价值的
wild	[waɪld] *adj.* 野生的
acceptable	[ək'septəbl] *adj.* 可接受的
accurate	['ækjərət] *adj.* 准确的
affordable	[ə'fɔːdəbl] *adj.* 负担得起的
ambitious	[æm'bɪʃəs] *adj.* 有雄心的
archaeological	[ˌɑːkiə'lɒdʒɪkl] *adj.* 考古学的
artificial	[ˌɑːtɪ'fɪʃl] *adj.* 人造的; 虚伪的
blind	[blaɪnd] *adj.* 盲目的
central	['sentrəl] *adj.* 中心的
certain	['sɜːtn] *adj.* 必然的; 某一个
childish	['tʃaɪldɪʃ] *adj.* 幼稚的
comfortable	['kʌmftəbl] *adj.* 舒适的
compulsory	[kəm'pʌlsəri] *adj.* 强制性的
creative	[kri'eɪtɪv] *adj.* 创造性的
critical	['krɪtɪkl] *adj.* 批评的; 决定性的
dangerous	['deɪndʒərəs] *adj.* 危险的
dietary	['daɪətəri] *adj.* 饮食的
difficult	['dɪfɪkəlt] *adj.* 困难的

disabled	[dɪs'eɪbld] *adj.* 有缺陷的
distinctive	[dɪ'stɪŋktɪv] *adj.* 独特的
dull	[dʌl] *adj.* 迟钝的
durable	['djʊərəbl] *adj.* 持久的
dusky	['dʌski] *adj.* 昏暗的
efficient	[ɪ'fɪʃnt] *adj.* 高效的
electrical	[ɪ'lektrɪkl] *adj.* 电的
environmental	[ɪnˌvaɪrən'mentl] *adj.* 环境的
essential	[ɪ'senʃl] *adj.* 重要的
excellent	['eksələnt] *adj.* 极好的
expensive	[ɪk'spensɪv] *adj.* 昂贵的
global	['ɡləʊbl] *adj.* 全球的
impressive	[ɪm'presɪv] *adj.* 给人印象深刻的
inconvenient	[ˌɪnkən'viːniənt] *adj.* 不方便的
inside	[ˌɪn'saɪd] *adj.* 内部的
internal	[ɪn'tɜːnl] *adj.* 内部的
irrelevant	[ɪ'reləvənt] *adj.* 不相关的
medical	['medɪkl] *adj.* 医学的; 药的
minor	['maɪnə(r)] *adj.* 次要的; 较小的
moderate	['mɒdərət] *adj.* 温和的; 适度的

multiple	['mʌltɪpl] *adj.* 多重的；多样的	sweet	[swiːt] *adj.* 甜的
natural	['nætʃrəl] *adj.* 自然的	total	['təʊtl] *adj.* 全部的
		traditional	[trə'dɪʃənl] *adj.* 传统的
navigational	[,nævɪ'geɪʃənl] *adj.* 航行的	underwater	[,ʌndə'wɔːtə(r)] *adj.* 水下的
nervous	['nɜːvəs] *adj.* 紧张的	unimportant	[,ʌnɪm'pɔːtnt] *adj.* 不重要的
obedient	[ə'biːdiənt] *adj.* 服从的	unique	[ju'niːk] *adj.* 独一无二的
opposite	['ɒpəzɪt] *adj.* 相反的	valid	['vælɪd] *adj.* 有效的
optional	['ɒpʃənl] *adj.* 可选择的	academic	[,ækə'demɪk] *adj.* 学术的
oral	['ɔːrəl] *adj.* 口头的	accountable	[ə'kaʊntəbl] *adj.* 有责任的；可解释的
outside	[,aʊt'saɪd] *adj.* 外面的		
particular	[pə'tɪkjələ(r)] *adj.* 特别的	administrative	[əd'mɪnɪstrətɪv] *adj.* 管理的，行政的
portable	['pɔːtəbl] *adj.* 手提的		
quiet	['kwaɪət] *adj.* 安静的	agricultural	[,ægrɪ'kʌltʃərəl] *adj.* 农业的
random	['rændəm] *adj.* 随机的		
realistic	[,riːə'lɪstɪk] *adj.* 现实的	allergic	[ə'lɜːdʒɪk] *adj.* 过敏的
regional	['riːdʒənl] *adj.* 地区的	ancient	['eɪnʃənt] *adj.* 古老的
renewable	[rɪ'njuːəbl] *adj.* 可再生的；可更新的	annual	['ænjuəl] *adj.* 每年的
		anonymous	[ə'nɒnɪməs] *adj.* 匿名的
sensitive	['sensətɪv] *adj.* 敏感的	astronomical	[,æstrə'nɒmɪkl] *adj.* 天文的
smooth	[smuːð] *adj.* 光滑的	attractive	[ə'træktɪv] *adj.* 吸引人的
sticky	['stɪki] *adj.* 黏性的	automatic	[,ɔːtə'mætɪk] *adj.* 自动的
strict	[strɪkt] *adj.* 严格的	average	['ævərɪdʒ] *adj.* 平均的
sunken	['sʌŋkən] *adj.* 沉没的	bilingual	[,baɪ'lɪŋgwəl] *adj.* 双语的

biographical	[ˌbaɪə'græfɪkl] adj. 传记的	doubtful	['daʊtfl] adj. 可疑的
biological	[ˌbaɪə'lɒdʒɪkl] adj. 生物的	dramatic	[drə'mætɪk] adj. 急剧的
bony	['bəʊni] adj. 骨瘦如柴的	drunk	[drʌŋk] adj. 喝醉的
captive	['kæptɪv] adj. 被俘虏的	edible	['edəbl] adj. 可食用的
cardinal	['kɑːdɪnl] adj. 主要的	effective	[ɪ'fektɪv] adj. 有效的
cheerful	['tʃɪəfl] adj. 愉快的	elderly	['eldəli] adj. 老年的
choppy	['tʃɒpi] adj. 波涛汹涌的	emotional	[ɪ'məʊʃənl] adj. 情绪的
coastal	['kəʊstl] adj. 沿海的; 海岸的	entire	[ɪn'taɪə(r)] adj. 全部的
comprehensive	[ˌkɒmprɪ'hensɪv] adj. 综合的	exact	[ɪɡ'zækt] adj. 准确的
conditional	[kən'dɪʃənl] adj. 有条件的	excessive	[ɪk'sesɪv] adj. 过多的
confident	['kɒnfɪdənt] adj. 自信的	executive	[ɪɡ'zekjətɪv] adj. 管理的
constant	['kɒnstənt] adj. 不变的	extreme	[ɪk'striːm] adj. 极端的
controversial	[ˌkɒntrə'vɜːʃl] adj. 有争议的	familiar	[fə'mɪliə(r)] adj. 熟悉的
cooperative	[kəʊ'ɒpərətɪv] adj. 合作的	famous	['feɪməs] adj. 著名的
costal	['kɒstl] adj. 肋骨的	fantastic	[fæn'tæstɪk] adj. 极好的
cruel	['kruːəl] adj. 残忍的	faraway	['fɑːrəweɪ] adj. 遥远的
crystal	['krɪstl] adj. 水晶的	fatal	['feɪtl] adj. 致命的
daily	['deɪli] adj. 每天的	final	['faɪnl] adj. 最终的
democratic	[ˌdemə'krætɪk] adj. 民主的	fluid	['fluːɪd] adj. 流动的
deterrent	[dɪ'terənt] adj. 遏制的	foreign	['fɒrən] adj. 外国的
digestive	[daɪ'dʒestɪv] adj. 消化的	formal	['fɔːml] adj. 正式的
domestic	[də'mestɪk] adj. 国内的	formative	['fɔːmətɪv] adj. 形成的

fragile	['frædʒaɪl] *adj.* 脆弱的；易碎的	integral	['ɪntɪgrəl] *adj.* 完整的
fresh	[freʃ] *adj.* 新鲜的	intense	[ɪn'tens] *adj.* 强烈的
further	['fɜːðə(r)] *adj.* 进一步的	interactive	[,ɪntər'æktɪv] *adj.* 互动的
geographical	[,dʒiːə'græfɪkl] *adj.* 地理的	introductory	[,ɪntrə'dʌktəri] *adj.* 引导的，介绍的
geological	[,dʒiːə'lɒdʒɪkl] *adj.* 地质的	leisure	['leʒə(r)] *adj.* 空闲的；休闲的
golden	['gəʊldən] *adj.* 金色的	linguistic	[lɪŋ'gwɪstɪk] *adj.* 语言的
gradual	['grædʒuəl] *adj.* 逐渐的	lonely	['ləʊnli] *adj.* 寂寞的
grown	[grəʊn] *adj.* 长大的	lucky	['lʌki] *adj.* 幸运的
harmful	['hɑːmfl] *adj.* 有害的	massive	['mæsɪv] *adj.* 大量的；巨大的
hidden	['hɪdn] *adj.* 隐藏的	measurable	['meʒərəbl] *adj.* 可测量的
homesick	['həʊmsɪk] *adj.* 想家的	mechanical	[mə'kænɪkl] *adj.* 机械的；力学的
household	['haʊshəʊld] *adj.* 家庭的，家用的	memorable	['memərəbl] *adj.* 难忘的；值得纪念的
immediate	[ɪ'miːdiət] *adj.* 立即的；直接的	minimal	['mɪnɪml] *adj.* 最低的；最小的
impractical	[ɪm'præktɪkl] *adj.* 不现实的	modern	['mɒdn] *adj.* 现代的
industrial	[ɪn'dʌstriəl] *adj.* 工业的	moral	['mɒrəl] *adj.* 道德的
inefficient	[,ɪnɪ'fɪʃnt] *adj.* 低效的	nearby	[,nɪə'baɪ] *adj.* 附近的
influential	[,ɪnflu'enʃl] *adj.* 有影响的	nocturnal	[nɒk'tɜːnl] *adj.* 夜间的
initial	[ɪ'nɪʃl] *adj.* 最初的	normal	['nɔːml] *adj.* 正常的
inland	[,ɪn'lænd] *adj.* 内陆的	nutritional	[nju'trɪʃənl] *adj.* 营养的
innovative	['ɪnəveɪtɪv] *adj.* 创新的		

obvious	['ɒbviəs] adj. 明显的	professional	[prə'feʃnl] adj. 专业的；职业的
operational	[ˌɒpə'reɪʃənl] adj. 操作的	proficient	[prə'fɪʃnt] adj. 熟练的
organic	[ɔː'gænɪk] adj. 有机的；组织的	profitable	['prɒfɪtəbl] adj. 有利可图的；有益的
outdoor	['aʊtdɔː(r)] adj. 户外的	radical	['rædɪkl] adj. 激进的
overall	[ˌəʊvər'ɔːl] adj. 全部的	rare	[reə(r)] adj. 稀有的
overseas	[ˌəʊvə'siːz] adj. 海外的	reasonable	['riːznəbl] adj. 合理的
overweight	[ˌəʊvə'weɪt] adj. 超重的	rechargeable	[ˌriː'tʃɑːdʒəbl] adj. 可充电的
parasitic	[ˌpærə'sɪtɪk] adj. 寄生的	reflective	[rɪ'flektɪv] adj. 反映的；反思的
peaceful	['piːsfl] adj. 和平的；平静的	regular	['regjələ(r)] adj. 有规律的
phonic	['fɒnɪk] adj. 有声的，声音的	relative	['relətɪv] adj. 有关的
physical	['fɪzɪkl] adj. 物理的；身体的	remote	[rɪ'məʊt] adj. 遥远的
poisonous	['pɔɪzənəs] adj. 有毒的	repetitive	[rɪ'petətɪv] adj. 重复的
polytechnic	[ˌpɒli'teknɪk] adj. 多种工艺的	reusable	[ˌriː'juːzəbl] adj. 可再使用的
positive	['pɒzətɪv] adj. 积极的	rhetorical	[rɪ'tɒrɪkl] adj. 修辞的
precious	['preʃəs] adj. 宝贵的	robotic	[rəʊ'bɒtɪk] adj. 机器人的
precise	[prɪ'saɪs] adj. 精确的	salty	['sɔːlti] adj. 咸的；含盐的
predictable	[prɪ'dɪktəbl] adj. 可预言的	separate	['seprət] adj. 分开的
prevalent	['prevələnt] adj. 普遍的	significant	[sɪg'nɪfɪkənt] adj. 重要的
preventable	[prɪ'ventəbl] adj. 可预防的	simple	['sɪmpl] adj. 简单的
private	['praɪvət] adj. 私人的	slippery	['slɪpəri] adj. 滑的

smart	[smɑːt] *adj.* 聪明的; 智能的	typical	['tɪpɪkl] *adj.* 典型的
sociable	['səʊʃəbl] *adj.* 社交的	unacceptable	[ˌʌnək'septəbl] *adj.* 无法接受的
solid	['sɒlɪd] *adj.* 固体的; 坚固的	unclear	[ˌʌn'klɪə(r)] *adj.* 不清楚的
sour	['saʊə(r)] *adj.* 酸的	uncomfortable	[ʌn'kʌmftəbl] *adj.* 不舒服的
stable	['steɪbl] *adj.* 稳定的	uneasy	[ʌn'iːzi] *adj.* 不舒服的
statistic	[stə'tɪstɪk] *adj.* 统计的; 统计学的	uneven	[ʌn'iːvn] *adj.* 不平均的
stormy	['stɔːmi] *adj.* 有暴风雨的; 猛烈的	unhealthy	[ʌn'helθi] *adj.* 不健康的
		unpleasant	[ʌn'pleznt] *adj.* 不愉快的
stressful	['stresfl] *adj.* 紧张的	unpredictable	[ˌʌnprɪ'dɪktəbl] *adj.* 不可预测的
successful	[sək'sesfl] *adj.* 成功的		
sugary	['ʃʊgəri] *adj.* 含糖的; 甜的	unsystematic	[ˌʌnˌsɪstə'mætɪk] *adj.* 不系统的
superficial	[ˌsuːpə'fɪʃl] *adj.* 表面的; 肤浅的		
		urban	['ɜːbən] *adj.* 城市的
sustainable	[sə'steɪnəbl] *adj.* 可持续的	useless	['juːsləs] *adj.* 无用的
tailless	['teɪlləs] *adj.* 无尾的	usual	['juːʒuəl] *adj.* 通常的
technical	['teknɪkl] *adj.* 技术上的	visible	['vɪzəbl] *adj.* 看得见的
thorough	['θʌrə] *adj.* 彻底的	visual	['vɪʒuəl] *adj.* 视觉的
tight	[taɪt] *adj.* 紧的	voluntary	['vɒləntri] *adj.* 志愿的
transportable	[træn'spɔːtəbl] *adj.* 可运输的	wealthy	['welθi] *adj.* 富有的
		workable	['wɜːkəbl] *adj.* 可行的
trim	[trɪm] *adj.* 整齐的	worn	[wɔːn] *adj.* 疲倦的; 旧的
tropical	['trɒpɪkl] *adj.* 热带的		

initially	[ɪˈnɪʃəli] adv. 最初；首先	completely	[kəmˈpliːtli] adv. 完全地
widely	[ˈwaɪdli] adv. 广泛地	directly	[dəˈrektli] adv. 直接地
easily	[ˈiːzəli] adv. 容易地	effectively	[ɪˈfektɪvli] adv. 有效地
immediately	[ɪˈmiːdiətli] adv. 立即	efficiently	[ɪˈfɪʃntli] adv. 高效地
mainly	[ˈmeɪnli] adv. 主要地	electronically	[ɪˌlekˈtrɒnɪkli] adv. 电子地
economically	[ˌiːkəˈnɒmɪkli] adv. 经济地	especially	[ɪˈspeʃəli] adv. 尤其
entirely	[ɪnˈtaɪəli] adv. 完全地	fairly	[ˈfeəli] adv. 相当地
monthly	[ˈmʌnθli] adv. 每个月	fully	[ˈfʊli] adv. 完全地
often	[ˈɒfn] adv. 常常	globally	[ˈɡləʊbəli] adv. 全球地
properly	[ˈprɒpəli] adv. 适当地	highly	[ˈhaɪli] adv. 非常地
rapidly	[ˈræpɪdli] adv. 迅速地	honestly	[ˈɒnɪstli] adv. 诚实地
recently	[ˈriːsntli] adv. 最近	mostly	[ˈməʊstli] adv. 通常
together	[təˈɡeðə(r)] adv. 一起；同时	never	[ˈnevə(r)] adv. 从不
actually	[ˈæktʃuəli] adv. 实际上	newly	[ˈnjuːli] adv. 最近
afterwards	[ˈɑːftəwədz] adv. 后来	normally	[ˈnɔːməli] adv. 通常地
ahead	[əˈhed] adv. 在前面	nowadays	[ˈnaʊədeɪz] adv. 如今；现在
always	[ˈɔːlweɪz] adv. 总是	occasionally	[əˈkeɪʒnəli] adv. 偶尔
annually	[ˈænjuəli] adv. 每年	originally	[əˈrɪdʒənəli] adv. 最初；起初
approximately	[əˈprɒksɪmətli] adv. 大约	particularly	[pəˈtɪkjələli] adv. 特别；尤其
briefly	[ˈbriːfli] adv. 简略地	physically	[ˈfɪzɪkli] adv. 身体上
carefully	[ˈkeəfəli] adv. 小心地	positively	[ˈpɒzətɪvli] adv. 乐观地

previously	['priːviəsli] *adv.* 以前	slowly	['sləuli] *adv.* 缓慢地
punctually	['pʌŋktʃuəli] *adv.* 准时地	spiritually	['spɪrɪtʃuəli] *adv.* 精神上地
quickly	['kwɪkli] *adv.* 迅速地	surprisingly	[sə'praɪzɪŋli] *adv.* 出人意料地
quite	[kwaɪt] *adv.* 很；相当		
randomly	['rændəmli] *adv.* 随机	thoroughly	['θʌrəli] *adv.* 彻底地
regularly	['reɡjələli] *adv.* 定期地；有规律地	virtually	['vɜːtʃuəli] *adv.* 事实上

（六）**常考搭配**

focus on	集中于	depend on	依赖于
in advance	提前	die out	灭绝；消失
pay attention to	注意	due to	由于
be known as	被认为是	feed on	以…为食
be made of	由…组成	go around	四处走动
give up	放弃	in the future	在将来
lack of	缺乏	lead to	导致
result in	导致	make sure	确保
be caused by	由…引起	rely on	依靠
be made into	被制成	switch off	关掉
book date	记账日	tend to	倾向于
change into	变成	a feeling of	…的感觉
be compared to	与…相比	a variety of	各种各样的
consist of	由…组成	account for	解释；导致；占…比例

agree on	对…取得一致意见	contribute to	贡献
all kinds of	各种各样的	convert into	转化
ask for	要求；寻找	deal with	处理
at once	立即，马上	derive from	来源于
at present	当前，现在	dozens of	几十；许多
at the top of	在首位；在顶端	drop off	减少；中途放下…；睡着
at weekends	在周末		
base on	基于	dry up	干涸
be able to	能够	eat out	外出吃饭
be attached to	附属于	except for	除…以外
be aware of	知道；意识到	extract from	提取
be close to	接近	go aboard	上船；上飞机
be covered with	充满	have nothing to do with	与…无关
be different from	与…不同		
be opposite to	与…相反	heat up	加热；升温
be proud of	为…而骄傲	high altitude	高海拔
be related to	与…有关	high quality	高品质
be satisfied with	满意于	high season	旺季
be suitable for	适合于	in detail	详细地
benefit from	得益于	in the form of	以…形式
bring on	导致	in the long run	从长远来看
carry out	执行；实施	keep fit	保持健康
		learn about	了解；学习

link to	连接	set up	建立；装配
live on	以…为生	settle down	定居
look after	照顾	show off	炫耀
look for	寻找	sign up	注册
out of control	失去控制	sort out	挑选出；分类
out of date	过时的；过期的	sound like	听起来像
part of	部分	take over	接管
peak season	旺季	the rest of	其余的；剩下的
pick up	捡起；学会	think about	思考；考虑
prevent from	阻止	turn to	转向；变成
problem solving	解决问题	wait for	等候
raise money	筹款	wake up	醒来
rather than	而不是	walk through	走过
refer to	提及；指的是…	work together	合作；共同工作
set out	出发；开始		

七 地名及相关词汇

大洲名称及相关词汇

Africa	['æfrɪkə] n. 非洲
Asia	['eɪʒə] n. 亚洲
Europe	['jʊərəp] n. 欧洲
Latin America	[ˌlætɪn ə'merɪkə] 拉丁美洲

North America	[ˌnɔːθ əˈmerɪkə] 北美洲
South America	[ˌsaʊθ əˈmerɪkə] 南美洲
African	[ˈæfrɪkən] *adj.* 非洲的 *n.* 非洲人
Asian	[ˈeɪʒn] *adj.* 亚洲的 *n.* 亚洲人
European	[ˌjʊərəˈpiːən] *adj.* 欧洲的 *n.* 欧洲人
Latin American	[ˌlætɪn əˈmerɪkən] 拉丁美洲的；拉丁美洲人
North American	[ˌnɔːθ əˈmerɪkən] 北美洲的；北美洲人
South American	[ˌsaʊθ əˈmerɪkən] 南美洲的；南美洲人

国家或地区名称及相关词汇

America	[əˈmerɪkə] *n.* 美国
Australia	[ɒˈstreɪliə] *n.* 澳大利亚
Britain	[ˈbrɪtn] *n.* 英国
Cambodia	[kæmˈbəʊdiə] *n.* 柬埔寨
Canada	[ˈkænədə] *n.* 加拿大
China	[ˈtʃaɪnə] *n.* 中国
England	[ˈɪŋɡlənd] *n.* 英格兰
France	[frɑːns] *n.* 法国
Germany	[ˈdʒɜːməni] *n.* 德国
Great Britain	[ˌɡreɪt ˈbrɪtn] *n.* 大不列颠，英国
Greece	[ɡriːs] *n.* 希腊
India	[ˈɪndiə] *n.* 印度
Indonesia	[ˌɪndəˈniːʒə] *n.* 印度尼西亚

Italy	['ɪtəli] *n.* 意大利	
Japan	[dʒə'pæn] *n.* 日本	
New Zealand	[ˌnjuː 'ziːlənd] *n.* 新西兰	
Nigeria	[naɪ'dʒɪəriə] *n.* 尼日利亚	
Poland	['pəʊlənd] *n.* 波兰	
Rome	[rəʊm] *n.* 罗马	
Russia	['rʌʃə] *n.* 俄罗斯	
Scotland	['skɒtlənd] *n.* 苏格兰	
Spain	[speɪn] *n.* 西班牙	
Sweden	['swiːdn] *n.* 瑞典	
Switzerland	['swɪtsələnd] *n.* 瑞士	
the North Pole	[ðə ˌnɔːθ 'pəʊl] 北极	
the South Pole	[ðə ˌsaʊθ 'pəʊl] 南极	
United States of America	[juˌnaɪtɪd ˌsteɪts əv ə'merɪkə] *n.* 美利坚合众国（美国）	
American	[ə'merɪkən] *adj.* 美国的 *n.* 美国人	
Australian	[ɒ'streɪliən] *adj.* 澳大利亚的 *n.* 澳大利亚人	
British	['brɪtɪʃ] *adj.* 英国的 *n.* 英国人	
Cambodian	[kæm'bəʊdiən] *adj.* 柬埔寨的 *n.* 柬埔寨人	
Canadian	[kə'neɪdiən] *adj.* 加拿大的 *n.* 加拿大人	
Chinese	[ˌtʃaɪ'niːz] *adj.* 中国的 *n.* 中国人	
English	['ɪŋglɪʃ] *adj.* 英国的 *n.* 英国人	
French	[frentʃ] *adj.* 法国的	

Frenchman	['frentʃmən] *n.* 法国人	
German	['dʒɜːmən] *adj.* 德国的 *n.* 德国人	
Greek	[griːk] *adj.* 希腊的 *n.* 希腊人	
Indian	['ɪndiən] *adj.* 印度的 *n.* 印度人	
Indonesian	[ˌɪndə'niːʒn] *adj.* 印度尼西亚的 *n.* 印度尼西亚人	
Italian	[ɪ'tæliən] *adj.* 意大利的 *n.* 意大利人	
Japanese	[ˌdʒæpə'niːz] *adj.* 日本的 *n.* 日本人	
New Zealander	[ˌnjuː 'ziːləndə(r)] *n.* 新西兰人	
Nigerian	[naɪ'dʒɪəriən] *adj.* 尼日利亚的 *n.* 尼日利亚人	
Polish	['pɒlɪʃ] *adj.* 波兰的 *n.* 波兰人	
Roman	['rəʊmən] *adj.* 罗马的 *n.* 罗马人	
Russian	['rʌʃn] *adj.* 俄罗斯的 *n.* 俄罗斯人	
Scottish	['skɒtɪʃ] *adj.* 苏格兰的 *n.* 苏格兰人	
Spanish	['spænɪʃ] *adj.* 西班牙的 *n.* 西班牙人	
Swedish	['swiːdɪʃ] *adj.* 瑞典的 *n.* 瑞典人	
Swiss	[swɪs] *adj.* 瑞士的 *n.* 瑞士人	

常考城市或地区

Alaska	[ə'læskə] *n.* 阿拉斯加州（美国最大的州）
Chicago	[ʃɪ'kaːgəʊ] *n.* 芝加哥（美国城市名）
London	['lʌndən] *n.* 伦敦（英国首都）
Northern Ireland	[ˌnɔːðən 'aɪələnd] 北爱尔兰自治区（位于爱尔兰东北部）

Oxford	['ɒksfəd] n. 牛津（英国城市）
Sydney	['sɪdni] n. 悉尼（澳大利亚港口城市）
Toronto	[tə'rɒntəʊ] n. 多伦多（加拿大城市）
Wales	[weɪlz] n. 威尔士（英国大不列颠岛西南部地区）
Wellington	['welɪŋtən] n. 惠灵顿（新西兰首都）
Bristol	['brɪstl] n. 布里斯托尔（英国西部的港口城市）
Venice	['venɪs] n. 威尼斯（意大利港市）
Washington D.C.	[ˌwɒʃɪŋtən ˌdiː 'siː] 华盛顿（美国首都）
Moscow	['mɒskəʊ] n. 莫斯科（俄罗斯首都）
New York City	[njuː jɔːk 'sɪti] 纽约（美国城市）

常考景点

Panama Canal	[ˌpænəmɑː kə'næl] 巴拿马运河
Disneyland	['dɪznilænd] n. 迪士尼乐园
Hyde Park	[ˌhaɪd 'pɑːk] 海德公园
Hollywood	['hɒliwʊd] n. 好莱坞
pyramid	['pɪrəmɪd] n. 金字塔
Las Vegas	[ˌlæs 'veɪgəs] n. 拉斯维加斯
Tower of London	[ˌtaʊər əv 'lʌndən] 伦敦塔
Yellowstone National Park	[ˌjeləʊstəʊn ˌnæʃnəl 'pɑːk] 美国黄石国家公园
Times Square	[ˌtaɪmz 'skweə(r)] 时代广场
Westminster Abbey	[ˌwestmɪnstər 'æbi] 威斯敏斯特大教堂

Central Park	[ˌsentrəl ˈpɑːk] 中央公园
Statue of Liberty	[ˌstætʃuː əv ˈlɪbəti] 自由女神像
Eiffel Tower	[ˈaɪfəl ˈtaʊə(r)] 埃菲尔铁塔
Great Barrier Reef	[greɪt ˈbæriə(r) riːf] 大堡礁
Mount Fuji	[maʊnt ˈfudʒi] 富士山
Sahara	[səˈhɑːrə] n. 撒哈拉沙漠
Suez Canal	[ˈsuːɪz kəˈnæl] 苏伊士运河
Taj Mahal	[tɑːdʒ mˈhɑːl] 泰姬陵
Victoria Falls	[vɪkˈtɔːrɪə fɔːlz] 维多利亚瀑布
Sydney Opera House	[ˈsɪdni ˈɒprə haʊs] 悉尼歌剧院

海洋名称

the Arctic Ocean	[ðə ˌɑːktɪk ˈəʊʃn] 北冰洋
the Atlantic Ocean	[ðə ətˌlæntɪk ˈəʊʃn] 大西洋
the Pacific Ocean	[ðə pəˌsɪfɪk ˈəʊʃn] 太平洋
the Indian Ocean	[ðə ˌɪndiən ˈəʊʃn] 印度洋
the Mediterranean Sea	[ðə ˌmedɪtəˈreɪniən siː] 地中海

02
CHAPTER

雅思听力
场景词汇

本章音频

雅思听力的所有题目都是在特定语境下对语言能力进行考查。这就意味着什么样的语境决定了音频中会出现什么样的信息，而这些信息决定了会出现什么样的题目。

在对语境的分类上，既可以按照形式进行划分，即分为对话和独白；也可以按照内容进行划分，即分为不同的场景。从词汇学习的角度而言，将词汇按场景分类对备考更加有效。对场景词的识别可以帮助考生理解听到的音频是围绕什么话题进行讨论的，以及预判音频中会出现哪些具体的单词和短语。

在实际考试中，场景词汇有两个主要作用。一个作用当然就是用来直接答题，因为最后选择的选项或者填入的单词往往就是重要的场景词，本章收录的场景词汇就是考试中要选择或填入的答案，这也会在很大程度上帮助考生提升备考效率。而另一个作用往往会被忽略，那就是帮助考生构建场景和激活大脑。当考生在听力中听到几个场景词后，大脑会自动构建一个场景，并且同时激活与之相关的场景词汇，产生"预期效应"，这对快速答题是非常重要的。而这种随着听力内容不断产生"预期"，并且随着后续内容不断验证和满足大脑预期的技能，也是具有不错的听力能力后获得的高级技能。想要获得更高的听力分数，这种能力是必须具备的。

第一节　住宿（Accommodation）

住宿是雅思听力考试中的经典场景，出现概率相当高。住宿场景在听力 Part 1 的考试内容主要包括两方面：咨询相关房屋或房间信息；个人信息的交换。

在日常练习和考试中，考生一定要关注对话双方的关系，如房东（landlord）、房客（tenant）和中介（house renting agency/agent），或者主房客（main tenant）和合租人（co-tenant）等。无论出租方还是承租方，都需要了解对方的个人信息，因此在对话中经常出现关于人名、住址等信息的提问与回答。房屋相关信息主要包括房屋本身介绍、房间类型、周边条件和租赁价格等。与此同时，与住宿相关的设施、家具用品等也是常考内容。对住宿场景相关词汇的熟练掌握也会对雅思口语相应话题的作答起到很大的帮助。

一 位置

location 位置

environment/surroundings 环境

city centre/central area/downtown 市中心

urban area 城市地区

rural area 农村地区

suburb/outskirt 郊区

countryside 乡下

road 路

street 街道

avenue 大道

lane 小巷

direction 方向

corner 角落

north 北；北方；朝北

south 南；南方；朝南

east 东；东方；朝东

west 西；西方；朝西

northern 北边的

southern 南边的

western 西边的

eastern 东边的

二 房屋类型

layout 布局

type of house 房屋类型

flat/apartment 公寓

studio apartment 单间公寓

hall of residence（英）宿舍

dormitory/dorm（美）宿舍

hotel 旅馆

motel 汽车旅馆

youth hostel 青年旅社

homestay 家庭寄宿

host family 寄宿家庭

guest house 招待所

standard suite 标准套间

bedsit 卧室兼起居室

single room 单人间

double room 双人间（一张床）

twin room 双人间（两张床）

三 人物

house agent 房地产经纪人

house agency 房屋中介

landlord/landlady 房东

property owner 业主

tenant 房客；租户

guest 客人

neighbour/neighbor 邻居

roommate/flatmate 室友

contact 联系方式

四 房屋及其设施

living room/sitting room 客厅

dining room 餐厅

shared kitchen 公用厨房

bathroom 浴室

toilet 厕所

water closet 盥洗室

cloakroom 衣帽间

wardrobe 衣橱

basement 地下室

garage 车库

garden 花园

courtyard 庭院

swimming pool 游泳池

balcony 阳台

corridor 走廊

attic 阁楼

cabin 小屋

car park 停车场

lobby/main hall 大厅

foyer 门厅

lounge 公共休息室

stereo system 立体声音响

refrigerator/fridge 冰箱

air conditioner 空调机

air conditioning 空调

heater 加热器

washing machine 洗衣机

shower 淋浴

vacuum cleaner 吸尘器

cooker 炊具

microwave oven 微波炉

drawer 抽屉

lift/elevator 电梯

cabinet 橱柜

fountain 喷泉

equipment 设备

facilities 房屋设施

electric fan 电扇

water heater 热水器

laundry room 洗衣房

radiator 暖气

dishwasher 洗碗机

stove 炉灶

toaster 烤面包机

fence 栅栏

furniture 家具

postbox 邮箱

ladder 梯子

tool 工具

五 家居用品

pillow 枕头

bed sheet 床单

quilt 棉被

carpet 地毯

cushion 沙发靠垫

towel 毛巾

mattress 床垫

blanket 毛毯

curtain 窗帘

sofa 沙发

lamp 灯

double-lock 上双锁

front door key 前门钥匙

pet 宠物

private property 个人财产

crack/split 裂开

leak 泄露

no smoking 禁止吸烟

fire gate/exit 紧急出口

contract 合同

noisy 吵闹的

privacy 隐私

七 费用

maximum rent 最高租金

minimum rent 最低租金

deposit 押金

utility bill 水电费

water bill 水费

electricity bill 电费

gas bill 煤气费

phone bill 电话费

refundable 可退还的

insurance 保险

rental price 房租价格

第二节 饮食（Food and Drink）

　　饮食场景词汇可以单独被考查，也可以融入其他的语境被考查。对饮食话题单独考查的例子有：有关旅行服务的介绍中专门针对饮食的讨论。而在其他场景中，比如在租房和兼职的场景中对个人饮食习惯（special diet）的询问和交流，或者在关于烹饪课程

（cooking courses）的讨论中出现饮食场景词汇。因此要注意每一类场景不一定是完全孤立的，也可能在一类场景中讨论到另一类场景的问题。

对于饮食类场景词，要格外注意同音异形词和发音相近词，尤其是在拼写的时候不能混淆。例如，flour（面粉）和 flower（花朵）、dessert（甜品）和 desert（抛弃）、snack（小食）和 snake（蛇）、coffee（咖啡）和 café（咖啡馆）、steak（牛排）和 stick（木棍）等。

一 地点

dining hall 食堂	restaurant 餐厅
café 咖啡馆	cafeteria 自助餐厅
buffet 自助餐	pub 酒吧
bakery 面包店	snack bar 小吃店
salad bar 沙拉吧	take-away 外卖

二 饮料

drink/beverage 饮料	alcohol 酒；酒精
wine 葡萄酒	cocktail 鸡尾酒
coffee 咖啡	tea 茶
mineral water 矿泉水	fruit juice 果汁
coke 可乐	yogurt/yoghurt 酸奶

三 食物及餐具

catering service 餐饮服务	refreshment/snack 小吃
main course 主菜	side dish 配菜

soup 汤

cuisine 烹饪

carrot 胡萝卜

lettuce 生菜

onion 洋葱

junk food 垃圾食品

pork 猪肉

lamb 羊肉

bacon 培根

ham 火腿

crab 螃蟹

lobster 龙虾

hamburger 汉堡包

sandwich 三明治

bread 面包

fish and chips 炸鱼薯条

apple pie 苹果馅饼

cheese 奶酪

flour 面粉

red pepper 辣椒

pumpkin 南瓜

watermelon 西瓜

dessert 甜点

vegetable 蔬菜

cucumber 黄瓜

mushroom 蘑菇

cabbage 卷心菜

meat 肉类

beef 牛肉

chicken 鸡肉

steak 牛排

turkey 火鸡

shrimp 虾

oyster 牡蛎

hotdog 热狗

pizza 比萨饼

noodle 面条

pudding 布丁

biscuit/cookie 饼干

chocolate bar 巧克力棒

corn 玉米

bean 豆

salad 沙拉

strawberry 草莓

jam 果酱

sugar 糖

curry 咖喱

butter 黄油

delicious/tasty 美味的

salty 咸的

bitter 苦的

menu 菜单

bowl 碗

knife 小刀

tissue/napkin 餐巾

sauce 酱汁

nut 坚果

honey 蜂蜜

balanced diet 均衡的饮食

spicy 辛辣的

sour 酸的

smelly 臭的

plate 碟子

fork 叉子

spoon 汤勺

四 饮食习惯

special diet 特殊饮食

food allergy 食物过敏

seafood 海鲜

peanut 花生

vegetarian 素食主义者

be allergic to 对…过敏

red meat 红肉（牛肉、羊肉等）

dairy product 乳制品

第三节 旅游（Travel）

　　旅游场景在雅思听力考试的 Part 1 和 Part 2 中比较常见，一般会涉及旅游前的话题和对旅游本身的描述。Part 1 中出现较多的是有关旅游前的话题，比如对旅行的咨询或者介绍。无论是自由行（independent tour）还是跟团旅游（package tour），都需要了解目的地的一些情况，如景点类型（tourist attraction / tourist resort / scenic spot / historical interest）及其特点、活动（activities）、注意事项（considerations）、衣物（clothes）、药品（medicine）等。除此之外，和旅行密切相关的票务、酒店预定（reservation）也是常考考点。在 Part 2 中考查的和旅游本身相关的场景词汇较多，一般会和游景点介绍有关，比如场地介绍、活动介绍、接送服务（pick-up and drop-off）、保险业务（insurance）等。

一　目的地

destination 目的地	U.K./the United Kingdom/Great Britain 英国
England 英格兰	Scotland 苏格兰
Wales 威尔士	Northern Ireland 北爱尔兰
London 伦敦	Australia 澳大利亚
Sydney 悉尼	New Zealand 新西兰
Canada 加拿大	Toronto 多伦多
United States of America 美国	New York 纽约
Washington D.C. 华盛顿	Chicago 芝加哥
Great Barrier Reef 大堡礁	Central Park 纽约中央公园
Sydney Opera House 悉尼歌剧院	Tower of London 伦敦塔

二 活动

tour/travel/trip/journey 旅行

tourism 旅游业

travel agency 旅行社

tour guide 导游

guided tour 带导游的旅行

schedule 时间表

package tour 跟团旅游

self-drive tour 自驾行

cruise 乘船巡游

helicopter trip 直升机旅行

mileage 里程数

adventure 探险

picnic 野餐

camping 野营

campsite 营地

cycling route 骑车路线

sight-seeing 观光

shopping 购物

rock climbing 攀岩

hiking 徒步旅行

surfing 冲浪

bush walk 丛林漫步

drifting 漂流

horse riding 骑马

fishing 钓鱼

survival course 野外生存课程

massage 按摩

cookery lesson 烹饪课

balloon ride 乘坐热气球

weather observation 观测天气

charity event 慈善活动

三 注意事项

noticeboard 公告栏

safety regulation 安全规章

emergency contact person 紧急联系人

personal belonging 个人物品

nationality 国籍

embassy 大使馆

passport 护照

identification card/ID card 身份证

driving license 驾照

thief 小偷

risk 风险

sharp corner 急转弯

accident 事故

rescue 救援

safety helmet 安全头盔

alarm system 警报系统

tropical disease 热带疾病

thunderstorm 雷雨

radio 无线电广播节目

Internet access 上网；互联网访问

wifi 无线网

information centre 信息中心

rule/regulation 规定

四 携带物品

walking boots 步行靴

comfortable clothes 舒适的衣服

map 地图

leaflet/booklet 小册子

tourist brochure 游客手册

souvenir 纪念品

digital camera 数码相机

video camera 录像机

compass 指南针

first aid kit 急救箱

sleeping bag 睡袋

life jacket 救生衣

rope 绳索

string 弦

wire 电线

gloves 手套

telescope 望远镜

torch/flashlight 手电筒

sunscreen/sun block/sun cream 防晒霜

lip balm 唇膏

mosquito net 蚊帐

sandals 凉鞋

bottled water 瓶装水

rain boots 雨鞋

smartphone 智能手机

stamp 邮票

tent 帐篷

sunglasses 太阳镜

raincoat 雨衣

rubber shoes 橡胶鞋

telegraph 电报

五 交通出行

make a reservation 预订

in advance/ahead of time 提前

confirm 确认

one-way ticket 单程票

round-trip ticket 往返票

canoe 独木舟

delay 延迟

traffic 交通

bus stop 车站

express train 特快列车

coach 长途客运汽车

cab/taxi 出租车

shuttle bus 班车；区间车

caravan 大篷车

book a ticket 订票

book online 网上预订

cancel 取消

single ticket 单程票

motorcycle 摩托车

steam engine ship 蒸汽船

transportation 交通方式

vehicle 车辆

railway station 火车站

minibus 小型巴士

ferry 轮渡

plane 飞机

double-decker bus 双层巴士

minivan 小型货车

lorry/truck 卡车

tram 电车

cable car 缆车

timetable 时刻表

duty-free shop 免税店

first class 头等舱

economy class 经济舱

arrival 到达

check in 办理登记手续

wheel 车轮

brake 刹车

platform 站台

hitch-hike 搭便车

bicycle 自行车

tube/metro/underground/subway 地铁

return ticket 往返票

airport 机场

direct flight 直达航班

business class 商务舱

departure 出发

vacant seat 空座

rush hour/peak time 交通高峰期

engine 发动机

wheelchair 轮椅

pick-up point 接人地点；上客访点

六 旅游景点

location/position/site/spot 地点

country 国家 / 乡村

village 村庄

lookout point 瞭望台

landmark 地标

waterfall 瀑布

cinema 电影院

region/area 地区

cottage 村舍

town 小镇

scenery/view/landscape/sight 风景

historical interest 名胜古迹

museum 博物馆

church 教堂

art gallery 美术馆

safari park 野生动物园

desert 沙漠

hot spring 温泉

beach 海滩

castle 城堡

ancient temple 古庙

bridge 桥

wetland 湿地

playground 运动场

workshop 车间

agriculture fair 农业集市；农艺展

craft shop 工艺店

post office 邮局

amusement park 游乐园

organic farm 有机农场

harbour/harbor 海港

bay 海湾

exit 出口

gift shop 礼品店

pyramid 金字塔

mountain 山脉

tunnel 隧道

canal 运河

cave 洞穴

palace 宫殿

island 岛

tropical rainforest 热带雨林

marsh 沼泽

pottery factory 瓷器工厂

old jail/prison 老监狱

town hall/city hall 市政厅

conference centre 会议中心

aquarium 水族馆

theme park 主题公园

coastal area 沿海地区

port 港口

main entrance 主入口

ticket office 售票处

七 人物

tourist/traveler/traveller 旅客

passenger 乘客

backpacker 背包客

family 家庭

child/children/kid 儿童

the elderly/the old 长辈

parents 父母

grandparent 祖父母

adult 成人

teenager 青少年

partner/spouse 配偶

offspring 后代

sibling 兄弟姐妹

cousin 同辈表亲（或堂亲）；远亲

aunt 阿姨；姑妈；伯母；舅妈

uncle 叔叔；伯父；舅舅；姨父；姑父

八 费用

fare/fee/expense/spending 费用

payment 付款

check/cheque 支票

traveller's check 旅行支票

cash 现金

credit 赊账

credit card 信用卡

Master Card 万事达卡

Visa Card 维萨卡

transfer 转账

currency 货币

dollar 美元 ($)

pound 英镑 (£)

euro 欧元 (€)

refund 退款

price list 价目表

change 零钱

extra charge 额外费用

accommodation package 住宿套餐

special offer 特价优惠

cancellation 取消

go Dutch/split the bill 各自付账，AA 制

第四节 健康（Health）

一般而言，健康场景经常出现在雅思听力考试的 Part 4 中。这类场景往往以独白的形式出现，由一名大学教授或专家开展有关健康问题的讲座，内容比较广泛，涉及营养学、两性健康等话题。

这类讲座在词汇和句型上会出现一些考生不太熟悉的内容，例如专业词汇、省略句和倒装句等。尽管录音中会出现有难度的词汇和复杂的句子，但题目本身和答案一般不会涉及专业知识，尤其是填入的答案，往往是常用的场景词汇。因此这一部分考查的重点是考生在关键信息定位、原文理解、单词辨音以及答案拼写方面的能力。

一 症状

symptom 症状

catch a cold 感冒

cough 咳嗽

fever 发烧

headache 头痛

stomachache 胃痛

toothache 牙痛

sore throat 嗓子疼

stuffed nose 鼻塞

stiff neck 脖子僵硬

back trouble 背痛

dizzy 头晕的

allergy 过敏

二 疾病

epidemic 流行病

flu 流感

heart disease 心脏病

injury 损伤

wound 伤口

scar 伤疤

tropical disease 热带病

chest infection 胸部感染

diarrhoea/diarrhea 腹泻

bad eyesight 糟糕的视力

bacteria 细菌

poison/toxin 毒素

disturbing 令人不安的

yellow fever 黄热病

pneumonia 肺炎

decayed tooth 蛀牙

disabled 残疾的

virus 病毒

poisonous/toxic 有毒的

memory 记忆

三 医院及医护

hospital 医院

health centre 健康中心

make an appointment 预约

physician 内科医生

dentist 牙医

nurse 护士

medical centre 医疗中心

clinic/practice 诊所

surgeon 外科医生

practitioner 执业医生

vet 兽医

patient 患者

四 身体

forehead 额头

neck 脖子

elbow 肘部

palm 手掌

knee 膝盖

mouth 嘴

shoulder 肩膀

wrist 手腕

finger 手指

toe 脚趾

chin/jaw 下巴

waist 腰部

ankle 脚踝

nail 指甲

lung 肺

kidney 肾脏

bone 骨头

brain 大脑

cell 细胞

mental 精神的

physical 肉体的

blood flow 血流

五 治疗

diagnose 诊断

treatment 治疗

therapy 疗法

physical therapy 理疗

precaution/prevention 预防

heart rate 心率

blood pressure 血压

pulse 脉搏

prescribe 开处方

injection 注射

vaccinate 注射疫苗

surgery 外科手术

operation 手术

ambulance 救护车

X-ray X 光

六 药物

drug store/pharmacy/chemist's 药店

medicine 药物

pill 药丸

tablet 药片

capsule 胶囊

painkiller 止痛片

vitamin 维生素

antibiotics 抗生素

eye drops 眼药水

herb 草药

nutrition 营养

protein 蛋白质

side effect 副作用

第五节　社会生活（Social Life）

　　社会生活场景主要包含运动、购物、娱乐和服装等话题。运动场景通常发生在健身房（gym/fitness center/sports club）的前台（reception），内容往往是咨询办卡或询问会员信息。不同的健身房有不同的运动设施（facilities）和课程（courses/training sessions），在这个场景中经常会提到会员制度（membership scheme）和办卡流程（card application）。购物相关话题可分为购物前和购物后。购物前主要是对商品的介绍，如价格（price）、材质（material）、颜色（colour）、功能作用（functions）等；购物后主要是对产品的反馈（feedback），如需要索赔（refund）、退货（return）等。索赔、退货的场景中经常出现产品信息的核对，如对品牌（brand）、型号（model）、价格（price）、购买时间（purchasing date）等的核对。考生要特别关注对产品问题的描述，录音中有时还会在达成一致意见后，要求留下个人信息，方便后续联系。

 运动

interest/hobby 爱好

membership 会员资格

joining fee 入会费

coach/instructor/trainer 教练

team leader 领队

judge 评委

bowling 保龄球

football 足球；橄榄球

soccer 足球

volleyball 排球

basketball 篮球

golf 高尔夫

snow-boarding 滑板滑雪

skiing 滑雪

water-skiing 滑水

roller-skating 旱冰

swimming 游泳

jogging 慢跑

yoga 瑜伽

stretch 伸展

kick-boxing 自由搏击

weight training 力量训练

baseball 棒球

hockey 曲棍球

tennis 网球

table tennis 乒乓球

badminton 羽毛球

squash 壁球

chess 国际象棋

sports centre/sports complex 体育馆

keep-fit studio/fitness club/gym 健身房

stadium 露天体育场

Olympics 奥运会

购物

shopping mall 购物中心

department store 百货商店

grocery store 杂货店

convenience store 便利店

purchase 购买

customer/client 顾客

consumer 消费者

reasonable price 合理的价格

annual fee 年费

budget 预算

subscription 订阅

retail chain 连锁店

best buy 最值得购买的产品

discount/on sale 打折

receipt 收据

invoice 发票

price tag 价格标签

label 标签

promotion 促销

display 展示

checklist 清单

shopping online 网上购物

website 网站

blog 博客

shop assistant 售货员

single item 单件物品

demand 需求

supply 供给

perfume 香水

cigar 雪茄

娱乐

leisure/recreation/entertainment 娱乐

relaxation 放松

movie theatre/cinema 电影院

comedy 喜剧

tragedy 悲剧

documentary 纪录片

cartoon 卡通片

science fiction movie 科幻片

sound effect 声效

subtitle 字幕

audience 观众

headphone 头戴式耳机

microphone 麦克风

exhibition 展览

dance studio 舞蹈工作室

stage 舞台

rehearse 排练

poster 海报

holiday/vacation 度假

traditional 传统的

outdoor activity 户外活动

decoration balloon 装饰气球

carnival 狂欢节

parade 游行

music festival 音乐节

concert hall 音乐厅

band 乐队

musical instrument 乐器

keyboard 键盘

piano 钢琴

pianist 钢琴家

string instrument 弦乐器

violin 小提琴

cello 大提琴

cellist 大提琴家

guitar 吉他

flute 笛子

clarinet 单簧管

trumpet 喇叭

drum 鼓

jazz music 爵士乐

clubhouse 俱乐部会所

四 服装

dress code 着装要求

costume 服装

formal clothes 正装

casual clothes 休闲装

dark trousers 深色裤子

skirt 短裙

sweater 毛衣

sportswear 运动装

uniform 制服

suit 西装

swimming suit 游泳衣

fabric 织物

textile 纺织品

fashionable 时髦的

satisfactory 令人满意的

fancy dress 舞会服装

silver cloth 银色布料

clothing 服装

jeans 牛仔裤

spare socks 备用袜子

texture 质地

pattern 图案

average 均码的

cotton 棉花

wool 羊毛	leather 皮革
velvet 天鹅绒	silk 丝绸
model 款式	stripe 条纹
blonde/blond 金发的	curved 弯曲的

第六节　工作（Work）

　　在雅思听力考试中，对工作场景的考查频率虽然不如旅游和住宿等场景高，但也是听力考试中的重要场景之一。工作场景中经常出现的是关于兼职工作的询问或者讨论某公司的招聘信息。

　　工作场景中的考查内容非常贴近真实生活，一般会涉及应征岗位（vacancy or position）、工作地点（workplace）、公司名称（专有名词的考查）、面试（interview）、公司福利待遇（如工资 pay/salary/wage、养老金 pension、假期 holiday/vacation 等）、工作时间（working time/shift）、部门（department/division）、培训（training）或工作职责（responsibility）、着装（dressing）等内容。

一　工作类型

occupation 职业	employment 就业
employer 雇主	employee 雇员
self-employed 个体经营的	staff 职员
director 主管；导演	actor/actress 演员
police officer 警察	project manager 项目经理
programmer 程序员	office assistant 办公室助理

waiter/waitress 服务员

designer 设计师

engineer 工程师

carpenter 木匠

hairdresser 理发师

receptionist 接待员

accountant 会计师

craftsman 工匠

journalist 记者

cleaner 清洁工

二 工作要求

job responsibility 工作职责

vacancy/vacant position 职位空缺

job applicant 工作申请人

job interview 面试

interviewee 面试者

part-time job 兼职工作

temporary staff 临时雇员

commuter 通勤者

experienced 经验丰富的

personality 性格

communication skill 交流能力

emotion/mood 情绪

respect 尊重

job arrangement 工作安排

think quickly 思维敏捷

tidy 整洁的

job duties 工作职责

recruit 招聘

CV/resume 简历

interviewer 面试官

full-time job 全职工作

permanent staff 固定人员

frequency 频率

academic background 学术背景

leadership 领导能力

social ability 社交能力

attitude 态度

confidence 自信

certificate 证书

qualification 品质

clear voice 口齿清晰

三 薪金待遇

benefit/welfare 福利

salary/wage/income 工资；收入

insurance policy 保单

medical insurance 医疗保险

opportunity for promotion 晋升空间

colleague 同事

coffee break 茶歇

time-off/day off 休息

tip 小费

paid vacation 带薪休假

flexible working time 弹性工作制

day shift 白班

night shift 晚班

四 银行

domestic bank 国内银行

overseas bank 国外银行

commercial bank 商业银行

merchant bank 商业银行

open an account 开户

current account 活期存款账户

deposit account 定期存款账户

joint account 联名账户

application form 申请表

identity certificate 身份证明

service charge 服务费 / 手续费

coin 硬币

penny 便士（复数 pence）

value/worth 面值

opening sum 开户金额

balance 账户余额

valid 有效的

security 安全性

bank statement 银行对账单

annual interest rate 年利率

low-interest loan 低息贷款

signature 签名

draw/withdraw 提款

exchange rate 汇率

password/passcode 密码

overdraw/overdraft 透支

mortgage 抵押

debt 债务

第七节 教育（Education）

　　教育场景涵盖各类学科、课程、入学和学习过程中可能遇到的问题（problem）、作业或论文讨论（discussion of assignments and papers）以及图书馆（library）等相关内容。图书馆是教育场景中比较重要的话题，很大原因是因为图书馆本身就是学习生活不可缺少的一部分，小组讨论（group discussion）、课程论文（coursework）、考试准备（exam preparation）这些学习任务大都需要利用图书馆的丰富资源来完成。图书馆场景在听力考试各个 Part 中都有可能出现，内容也各不相同。在 Part 1 中出现的图书馆场景以办理借书证及介绍图书馆的基本功能为主，经常出现有关个人信息和借阅信息的内容，比如学生的身份、所借书籍类别、借书期限等。剑 6–Test 4–Part 3 考查了参考书（reference）、逾期未归还书籍（overdue book）、过期刊物（back issue）的拼写，还提及召回图书（recalled book）、图书馆资源（library resource）、论文会议（dissertation convention）等词汇。如果考生对这类场景词汇不熟悉，在考试中出错的概率会非常大。

　　此外，教育场景题目还可能涉及培训课程，比如兼读课程（part-time course）、模块化课程（modular course）等。这类场景也会经常考查课程要求（course requirement）、作业类型（assignment type）、截止日期（deadline）、阅读书目（reading list）、学费（tuition fee）等方面的信息。

 学科

major 主修

minor 辅修

subject/discipline 学科

liberal arts 文科

science 理科

fine arts 美术

mathematics/maths 数学

accountancy/accounting 会计学

architecture 建筑学

anthropology 人类学

astronomy 天文学

biology 生物学

chemistry 化学

computer science 计算机科学

engineering 工程学

economics 经济学

finance 金融学

geography 地理

history 历史

journalism 新闻学

linguistics 语言学

literature 文学

mass media 大众传媒

politics 政治

physics 物理学

physical education (PE) 体育

psychology 心理学

statistics 统计学

 人物

president/principal/headmaster 校长

dean 系主任

secretary 秘书

professor 教授

associate professor 副教授

lecturer/instructor 讲师

supervisor 指导老师

tutor 导师

teaching assistant 助教

counselor 顾问

coordinator 协调员

faculty/office staff 教职员工

student advisor 学生顾问

candidate 候选人

representative 代表

international/overseas student 国际学生

freshman（大学）一年级学生

sophomore（大学）二年级学生

junior（大学）三年级学生

senior（大学）四年级学生

semester/term 学期

orientation week 新生入学周；迎新周

compulsory course 必修课

optional course 选修课

lecture 大班授课

tutorial 小班辅导课

speech 演讲

presentation 展示

seminar 研讨会

workshop 讲习班

group discussion 小组讨论

experiment 实验

beginning course 入门课程

basic course 基础课

intermediate course 中级课程

advanced course 高级课程

intensive course 强化课

training session 培训课

modular course 模块课程

Academic English Studies 学术英语研究

tape recorder 磁带录音机

projector 投影仪

handout 课堂讲义

primary school/elementary school 小学

secondary school 中学

college/university 大学

undergraduate 本科生

postgraduate 研究生

certificate 证书

diploma 学位证书

ceremony 典礼

Bachelor's degree 学士学位

Master's degree 硕士学位

Doctor's degree 博士学位

PhD/Doctor of Philosophy（哲学）博士

四 问题

registration 注册

enrollment fee 报名费

pressure/stress 压力

social network 社交圈

disruption 扰乱

regular exercise 定期练习

attention 注意力

inaccurate 不准确的

reliable source 可靠来源

support 支持

silent 沉默的

problem-solving 问题解决

note-taking skill 记笔记的能力

financial problem 经济问题

bullying 霸凌行为

dropout 辍学

time management 时间管理

technique 技巧

efficiency 效率

reasonable excuse 合理解释

confusion 困惑

necessary 必需的

五 评估

assignment/coursework 作业

written work 书面作业

task/mission 任务

case study 案例研究

achievement 成就

study diary 学习日记

feedback 反馈

evaluation 评估

assessment method 考核方法

excellent 卓越的

exam/examination 考试

quiz 小测验

failure 不及格

mark/score 分数

grade 成绩

record 记录

credit 学分

transcript 成绩单

detail 细节

priority 优先权

attendance rate 出勤率

absence 缺勤

 六 论文

paper 论文

essay 短文

thesis 专题论文

dissertation 毕业论文

report 报告

project 项目

subject 研究对象

topic/title 题目

final draft 终稿

outline 大纲

structure 结构

abstract 摘要

summary 总结

assumption 假设

objective/purpose 目标

research 研究

investigation/survey 调查

cover page 封面

contents page 目录页

literature review 文献综评

subheading 副标题

chapter/section 章节

paragraph 段落

format 格式

extension 延期

submit/hand in 提交

deadline 截止日期

graph 图表

proposal 提议

figure 数据

sample 样本

research method 研究方法

interview 采访

observation 观察

field trip 实地考察

questionnaire 问卷调查

collect data 收集数据

analysis 分析

measurement 测量

reference 参考书目

introduction 引言

previous study 以前的研究

relevant 相关的

common sense 常识

bibliography 参考文献目录

conclusion 结论

theoretical framework 理论架构

 七 图书馆

librarian 图书管理员

circulation desk 借书台

due-date 截止日期

loan period 可借书时间

recall 召回

category/classification 分类

current issue 现刊

book shelf 书架

printer 打印机

check out 登记借出

computer lab/computer centre 机房

media centre 媒体中心

multimedia material 多媒体资料

database 数据库

periodical 期刊

reception desk/counter 前台

student card 学生卡

overdue fine 过期罚金

renew 续借

reserve 预留

catalogue/catalog 分类目录

back issue 过期期刊

photocopier 复印机

scanner 扫描仪

self-access centre 自主学习中心

software 软件

computer terminal 计算机终端

publisher/press 出版社

author 作者

magazine 杂志

journal article 学术期刊

newspaper 报纸

fiction/novel 小说

textbook/course book 教材

videotape 录像带

card index 卡片索引

第八节 讲座（Lecture）

　　雅思听力的 Part 4 通常为学术讲座。这类题目文章长，信息量大，对考生的各方面能力要求比较高。讲座场景一般以独白形式出现，有时是校内老师或者校外专家向学生介绍各种知识，有时是学生演讲。比起其他三个部分，Part 4 的话题更丰富，有和生活相关的，也有和学术相关的。曾经出现在 Part 4 讲座的话题包括动物（animal）、植物（plant）、地理（geography）、地质（geology）、天文（astronomy）、生活健康（life and health）、经济（economics）、历史（history）、商业（business）、环境（environment）、教育（education）等。

　　Part 4 要求考生掌握的单词范围较广，并具备较广的知识面，尽力听懂整个讲座的主题和结构，并且边听讲座，边将听到的内容与试卷上的题目进行对应，填入考查的词汇。扎实地掌握场景词汇有助于在该部分获得满意分数。

一 商业

investment 投资

capital 资本

overhead 经费

takeover 收购

strike 罢工

stock market 股市

market share 市场份额

marketing strategy 营销策略

manufacture 厂商

campaign 活动

advertising 广告

logo 公司标识

sales figure 销售额

profit 利润

tax/taxation 税

production 生产

cost control 成本控制

expansion 扩张

consumption 消费

warehouse/storehouse 仓库

competition 竞争

cooperation 合作

corporation/firm/company 公司

corporate crime 公司犯罪

import 进口

export 出口

industry 工业

factory 工厂

aspiration/ambition 抱负

innovation 创新

creative 创造性的

vision 远见

democratic 民主的

superiority 优越性

update 更新

complex/complicated 复杂的

mediator 调停者

环境

atmosphere 大气

climate change 气候变化

ecosystem 生态系统

air quality 空气质量

greenhouse effect 温室效应

global warming 全球变暖

temperature 温度

oxygen 氧气

carbon dioxide 二氧化碳

ozone layer 臭氧层

emission 排放

rainfall 降雨

evaporate 蒸发

ocean currents 洋流

fog 雾

weather 天气

windy 有风的

rainy 有雨的

snowy 有雪的

cloudy 多云的

humid/moist/wet 潮湿的

shady 有树荫的

alternative energy 可替代能源

renewable resources 可再生资源

predictable 可预测的

filter 过滤

pollution/contamination 污染

pollutant/contaminant 污染物

rubbish/garbage/trash 垃圾

waste disposal 垃圾处理

plastic collection 塑料回收

recycling material 回收材料

container 容器

erosion 侵蚀

damage/destruction 破坏

acid rain 酸雨

volcano eruption/volcanic eruption 火山喷发

flood 洪水

drought 干旱

influence/impact 影响

hunting 打猎

deforestation 森林砍伐

solution 解决办法

international cooperation 国际合作

public awareness 公众意识

constant supply 持续供应

sustainable development 可持续发展

protection/conservation/preservation 保护

资源和材料

coal 煤

metal 金属

iron 铁

mine 矿

mineral 矿物质

marble 大理石

firewood 柴火

petrol/gasoline 汽油

tide 潮汐

natural resources 自然资源

water treatment 水处理

nuclear power plant 核电站

crystal 晶体

timber 木材

liquid 液体

oil 油类

solar energy/solar power 太阳能

wind force 风力

raw material 原材料

electric power plant 发电厂

fossil fuel 化石燃料

fiberglass 玻璃纤维

solid 固体

四 地理及其他

geographical feature 地理特征

planet 行星

plain 平原

traffic density 交通密度

technology 技术

Antarctica 南极洲

dweller/inhabitant 居民

race 种族

lifestyle 生活方式

slang 俚语

satellite 卫星

Earth surface 地表

comet 彗星

cliff 悬崖

distortion 扭曲

monitor 监控

population 人口

minority 少数民族

slave 奴隶

language 语言

culture 文化

wildlife 野生动物

rare breed animal 稀有动物

creature 生物

gene pool 基因库

diversity/variety 多样性

ancestor 祖先

threaten 威胁

endangered species 濒危物种

extinct species 灭绝物种

mammal 哺乳动物

reptile 爬行动物

snake 蛇

dinosaur 恐龙

crocodile 鳄鱼

kangaroo 袋鼠

zebra 斑马

elephant 大象

lion 狮子

wolf 狼

fox 狐狸

deer 鹿

goose 鹅（*pl.* geese）

marine animal 海洋动物

shark 鲨鱼

dolphin 海豚

whale 鲸鱼

insect 昆虫

honey bee 蜜蜂

butterfly 蝴蝶

spider 蜘蛛

pest 害虫

parasite 寄生虫

sting 蚊虫叮咬

migration pattern 迁徙模式

habitat 栖息地

nest 鸟巢

behaviour 行为

fur 皮毛

feather 羽毛

skeleton 骨骼

limb 四肢

bull 公牛

goat 山羊

crow 乌鸦

eagle 老鹰

tail 尾巴

wing 翅膀

cattle/livestock 家畜

owl 猫头鹰

scale 鱼鳞

fin 鱼鳍

breeding/reproduction 繁殖

六 植物

agriculture 农业

plant 植物

leaf 叶子（*pl.* leaves）

core 核

stem 茎

wood 木材

grain 谷物

artificial flower 人造花

grass 草

bloom/blossom 开花

gardening 园艺

irrigation 灌溉

clay 黏土

vegetation 植被

root 根

fruit 果实

seed 种子

branch 树枝

crop 农作物

bamboo 竹子

rose 玫瑰

weed 野草

forest 森林

cultivate 种植

soil 土壤

mud 泥

03

CHAPTER

听力同义
替换词表

本章音频

同义替换能力是贯穿雅思考试听、说、读、写四个单项的重要技能。在听力中具体的体现是听力原文中听到的词汇和题目中的词汇发生替换，使用不同的表达方式来表达相同的含义。本章总结的同义词均来自剑桥雅思听力真题，所有收录的同义替换词汇均为出题点。表格中题目词汇指在雅思听力题目中出现的词汇，原文词汇指题目词汇在听力原文文本中的对应表达。

　　需要注意的是，同义替换不完全等同于同义词。或者说，同义词只是同义替换的一种形式。不管是在日常表达还是雅思考试中，只要使用不同的方式表达了相同的含义，都可以被称为同义替换。具体来说，同义替换的表现形式有以下几种：

1. 同义词

　　例如，feature 和 characteristic 都表示"特征"，potential threat 和 possible danger 都表示"潜在危险"。这种本身含义相同的单词或短语的同义替换非常常见。

2. 包含关系

　　例如，container 表示"容器"，pot 表示"罐子"，罐子是容器的一种；animal 表示"动物"，livestock 表示"牲畜"，牲畜是动物的一类；official 表示"官员"，mayor and dignitary 表示"市长和高官"，它们都有"官员"的含义。这些都是通过对一个概念进行具体化来同义替换的。

3. 解释说明

　　例如，employee 表示"员工"，people who work there 表示"在那里工作的人"，这其实是对"员工"的解释。类似的例子还有 rapid promotion 和 quickly make one's way up the career ladder，前者表示"快速升职"，后者表示"迅速攀爬职业阶梯"；reduce traffic congestion 和 cut the number of cars on the road，前者表示"减少交通阻塞"，后者表示"减少道路上汽车的数量"。这些都是两个表达之间发生了同义替换。

题目词汇	原文词汇	解释
a great deal of	full of	大量；充满
a growth in sales	improve their sales figures	提升销量
a long way off	in the long-term future	长远
a lot of	considerable	相当多的
a means of	a form of	一种方式
a minimum of	at least	至少
a small number of	a few	少量的
a variety of/various	a range of	多样的
administrator	official	管理人员；官员
advantage	positive side	优点；积极的方面
affecting	disturbing	干扰的
affordable	economical	付得起的；经济的
ahead of time	in advance	提前
aim at	target at	把…定为目标
alone	single/without a partner	孤独；单独
alter	change/transform	改变
amounts	quantities	数量
ancestors	descend from	祖先；起源于

题目词汇	原文词汇	解释
ancient forts	medieval castles and fortifications	古堡；中世纪城堡和筑垒
animals	fauna/livestock/creatures	动物；动物群
another	alternative	另一个；供替代的选择
apprenticeship	being an apprentice	学徒
approximately	about	大约
area	field/space	领域；空间
arrange	make the arrangements	安排
as much variety as possible	wide range	多样
ask questions	check with someone	询问
available to the masses	accessible to the ordinary people	普通大众可获得的
back	return	返回
be aware of	be knowledgeable about	意识到；了解
be confused	get mixed up	混淆
be familiar with	know well	熟知
be included in the cost	no extra charge	无额外费用
be independent	be without parents	独立的；不和父母一起
be infested	carry	被寄生；携带
be interested in	passion for/be keen on	对…感兴趣；有热情
be postponed	be put on hold	推迟；搁置
be widened	make it wider	加宽

题目词汇	原文词汇	解释
begin	get started	开始
behind	back/at the back of	在…后面
better	superior/improved	更好的
bike tour	cycle trip	自行车旅行
bill	overheads	开支
bones	skeleton	骨头；骨骼
book	reserve	预定
books and journals	references	书和杂志；参考资料
build up	strengthen	加强

第二节　字母 C

题目词汇	原文词汇	解释
campaign	petitions and demonstrations	运动；请愿和游行
can be bought	be on sale	可以买的；在售的
caring	nurturing	照顾
cause	result in/lead to	造成
chance	coincidence/opportunity	机会；巧合
change	amend	修改
change back to	revert to	变回…
changing	shifting	变化的

题目词汇	原文词汇	解释
check	make amendments	检查；修改
childcare	babysitting	照顾小孩
chilled	cold	寒冷的
classified	category	分类
clear	definitive/obvious	明确的
climate change	global warming	气候变化；全球变暖
coastal cities	cities built by the sea	海边城市
color	tint	染色
communicate	keep in touch with	交流；联系
complete the form	fill in the form	填表
component	part/proportion	部分
comprehensive	full story	全面的；详细内容
compulsory	must	强制的；必须
conclusions	results	结论
confused	ambiguous	迷惑不清的
connected with	associated with	与…有关
constant supply	enough	供应充足
construct	make	建造
construction	build	建造
contact	get in touch with	联系
containers	cargoes	集装箱

题目词汇	原文词汇	解释
coordination	work together	合作
cosmetics	shampoo, soap	化妆品；洗发水、香皂
cost	fees	花费
cost a fortune	expensive	花大价钱；昂贵的
countryside	rural areas	乡村
create	design	创作
current	at present	现在的；现在
cut	shorten	减少

第三节　字母 D-F

题目词汇	原文词汇	解释
deforestation	cut down a large number of trees	滥砍滥伐
delay	hold-up	延迟
demand	order	命令
demonstration	performance	展示；表现
develop	improve	改进
difficult	be a problem	困难
difficult weather conditions	cold and windy	天气状况不佳；寒冷和多风的
difficulty	hardship	艰难困苦

题目词汇	原文词汇	解释
direct	first-hand	直接的；一手的
disappear	vanish	消失
discuss	talk about	谈论
discussions	consult	商讨；咨询
display	demonstration	展示
dispose	dump	扔
distinct	different	不同的
disturbing	noisy	引起烦恼的；吵闹的
diversity	variety	多样化
do not feel any real sense of satisfaction	dissatisfied	不满意
drive slowly	drive under 20 kilometres per hour	低速行驶；行驶速度低于 20 千米每小时
during the week	from Monday to Friday	一周内；周一到周五
earn	gain	赢得
eat	feed on	吃
elitist	minority	精英；少部分人
energetic	a lot of energy	有活力的
engine maintenance	mechanical work	机械维护工作
entertainment	amusement	娱乐
especially	in particular/particularly	特殊地
essential	have to	重要的；不得不…

题目词汇	原文词汇	解释
establish	built/set up/create	建立；创造
exact	precise	准确的
exceed	above	多于；在…之上
exercise	test	练习；测试
exhibition	display	展示
existing	available	现有的；可获得的
expect	assumption	预料；假设
explain	go through	解释；翻阅，彻查
export	be sold abroad	出口
extra charge	additional payment	额外费用
extreme environment	harsh weather conditions	极端环境；恶劣的天气情况
factories, warehouses and storehouses	industry	工业
fast movement	rapid motion	快速的动作
faster	more quickly	更快的；更快地
features	characteristics	特点
fewer/less	reduced	少的；减少的
finish	complete	完成
first person to do it	achieve it before anyone else	完成某事的第一人
fix onto	attach to	固定到…
flood prevention system	drainage channels	防洪系统；下水道

题目词汇	原文词汇	解释
focus on	emphasize	关注; 强调
footwear	shoes	鞋
for the first time	began	第一次; 开始
former	used to be	之前的
found	set up	建立
from the basics	at the beginning	从根本上; 起初
fully booked	no places left	全部订满
fun	enjoyable	有趣的

第四节 字母 G-I

题目词汇	原文词汇	解释
gate	entrance	门口; 入口
gift	present	礼物
give advice and guidance	very supportive	提供建议和指导; 十分支持的
give out	hand out	分发
given	donated	捐赠
gone	replace	消失; 代替
good value for money	not expensive	价格合适的
grow vegetables	plant vegetables	种植蔬菜
growth	expanding	扩大

题目词汇	原文词汇	解释
hard to understand	confusing	令人困惑的
hardly any	limited/little	很少
harm	frighten or injure	惊吓或伤害
have view of (the river)	look out at (the river)	朝向（小河）
heard	being told	听说
heavy traffic	busy roads	繁忙的交通
high temperatures	too hot	高温
homes	houses	房屋
hooves	feet	蹄子
humanoid	in the shape of a human	人形的
ice-skaters	people ice skating	滑冰的人
ideal	perfect	理想的；完美的
ideas	points/theories	观点；理论
identified	discovered	被发现的
imagine	visualize/picture	想象
immediate	straight away	立刻；马上
important	significant	重要的
impose	exert	实施
improve	refurbish/enhance	改善；翻新
improve air quality	reduce emissions on air pollution	提高空气质量

题目词汇	原文词汇	解释
in employment	working	工作中
in total	altogether	总体
increase in demand	a tremendous need	大量需求
increased dramatically	on a large scale	激增
induction	orientation	就职；迎新会
initial	at first	最初的，首先
injure	hurt	伤害
interpret	draw correct conclusions	阐明
interrupted	disruption	打断
introverted	shy	内向的
invent	develop	发明

第五节　字母 J-N

题目词汇	原文词汇	解释
jewels	precious stones	珠宝；宝石
just like	similar to	类似
keep active	stimulate	保持活跃；激活
keep fish	breed fish	养鱼
kept frozen	didn't melt	冻住的；没有融化的
knives and forks	cutlery	刀叉；餐具

题目词汇	原文词汇	解释
know	be informed of	知道；被告知
lack of water	dry out	缺水；干旱
land	field	土地
laptop	computer	电脑
large	massive/significant	大的；多的
large amounts of	a lot of	大量…，很多…
large global companies	major global corporations	大型跨国公司
last part	conclusion	结论
leading	most advanced	领先的
leave out	omit	省略，忽略
less noise	quieter	更安静的
less specific	not to be too precise	不太具体的；不太精确的
less suspicious	trust	信任
lessen	reduce	减少
lifestyles	ways in which we choose to live	生活方式
limit	restrict	限制
local	native to the region	当地的
local community	people living nearby	当地社区；当地居民
location	spot	地点
long time	considerable time	很长时间

题目词汇	原文词汇	解释
look	observe	看；观察
look after	supervise/watch over	照料；监督
low price	cheap	便宜
made of	constructed from	由…制成
maintain	keep	保持
make detailed notes	write down all the ideas	做详细的笔记；记下所有想法
make generalization	make a general conclusion	总结
make notes	note key information	记笔记
make sth from	make sth out of	用…制造某物
manageable	achievable	可达到的
manufacture	make	制造
manufacturing	production	生产
mayor and dignitaries	officials	官员
measure	provide in index	测量
media	press/journalism	媒体
meet	chat with	见到；和…聊天
metal industry	iron forge	金属工业；锻造炉
mineral water	drink	矿泉水；饮料
misunderstand	get the wrong idea	误解，误会
mites	parasites	寄生虫

题目词汇	原文词汇	解释
mix with	interact with	与…往来
more current	update	更新
more investment is required	not enough has been spent	需要更多投资
more than	over	多于
most popular	attract the largest number of visitors	最受欢迎的
mostly	mainly	主要地
motivate	inspire	激励
move into underground	buried	掩埋
move to a new location	reopen on a different site	换新址
move up	promotion	升职
nearly every	most/majority	大多数
neglect	not take into consideration	忽略
new types of	new sources of	新型的
newest	latest	最新的
no charge	free/no payment required	免费
not available	closed	不营业
not much	limited/restricted	少
not too bad	effective	不错的；有效的
not touch	stay at a safe distance	不要碰；远离
notices	signs	公告牌

题目词汇	原文词汇	解释
obey	follow	听从
occupation	job	工作
occurrence	outbreak	出现
of course	definitely	肯定
old	antique	古老的
on one hand, on the other hand	balance conflicting needs	一方面…另一方面…；平衡相互冲突的需求
one-on-one	individual	一对一的
online research	look at websites	浏览网站
opposite	on the other side of	在…对面
originally	the origin of	起初
out of bounds	not allowed	不允许
out of date/outdated	old-fashioned	过时的，老旧的
outgoing	sociable	外向的；好交际的
outline	structure	大纲
outside	exterior	外部的
owner	landlord	房东
particular	specific	特定的
people nearby	neighbors	邻居

题目词汇	原文词汇	解释
people of all ages	young and old	所有年龄的人
people who work there	employees	员工
performed by	is scored for	由…演奏
permanent	long-lasting	持久的
phase out	reduced	减少
phoning	calling	打电话
physical injury	vulnerable physically	身体受伤
plan for	make arrangements for	计划，安排
plants	vegetables	植物；蔬菜
pleased	happy	高兴的
plenty of	several	一些
pollutants	contaminants	污染物
pot	container	容器
potential threat	possible danger	潜在的危险
poverty	poor	贫穷；贫穷的
presented	be given	被给予
preserving	sustainable	持续的
priority	preference	优待；优先权
produce	create	生产；创造
prominent	put at the beginning	放在首位
protect	safeguard/save	保护

题目词汇	原文词汇	解释
provide	give	提供
publish in the media	see on TV or in the newspaper	媒体报道
pull	draw	拉
pull out	stop participating	退出
quite near	not far from	距离不远
quite soon	near future	不远

第七节　字母 R-S

题目词汇	原文词汇	解释
rapid	not slow	迅速的
rapid promotion	quickly make their way up the career ladder	快速晋升
rare	unusual	罕见的，不寻常的
realize	be cautious of	意识到
rebuild	reconstruct	重建
reclaimed	recycled	回收
recover	overcome its problems	恢复
recreation	leisure	空闲
reduce	lower	减少

题目词汇	原文词汇	解释
reduce stress	relax	放松
reduce traffic congestion	cut the number of cars on the road	减少交通拥堵
refurbish	redecorate	翻新，重新装饰
regularly	a few times a week	有规律地；一周几次
relocate	move to other parts	迁移；换址
require	need/the need for/demand	需要
research sources	books and websites	研究来源；书籍和网站
reservation	booking	预定
respect	esteem	尊重，尊敬
return to	back to	回去
rigorous	strict/more limited	严苛，限制
risky	too dangerous	危险
rounded	curvier	圆的
routine life	everyday lives	日常生活
sea	marine	海洋
senior roles	senior management positions	高级管理职位
share a room	twin room	分享房间；双人间
ship	ferrying	用船运输
shortage	not enough/lack of	不足；缺乏
show	prove	证明

题目词汇	原文词汇	解释
side access	separate entrance	侧门
similar	the same	一样，相似
simple	straightforward	简单的
slim	thin	瘦的
slow	take long time	慢
smaller than life size	miniature	微型的
snacks	food	零食；食物
solve problems	improve the situation	解决问题
some	a certain degree of	一些；一定程度的
sort	type	种类
stage	step	阶段
standard	fixed/normal	固定的，标准的
start	embark on/launch/have a go at	开始
statue	sculpture	雕像
stone statue	stone carving	石刻
stop	prevent	阻止
strategies	tactics	战术
struck	impressive	令人震惊的
studies	findings	发现；研究
study	learn to	学习

题目词汇	原文词汇	解释
stuff	things	东西
stylish	sleek/modern	时髦的
subject	topic/title	主题
sufficient	enough	充足的
summit	top	山顶
supply of water	water resources	水资源
surplus	more	过剩的；更多的
surprised	hadn't expected	预料之外
surprisingly	amazingly	令人惊讶地
surrounded by trees	get tress all around	被树环绕
survey	record	调查；记录
swim	dip in the ocean	游泳
switch it on	start	开机

第八节 字母 T-W

题目词汇	原文词汇	解释
take	last	持续
take away	removing	移除
take exercise	do activities	做运动
take place	happen	发生

题目词汇	原文词汇	解释
tall	high	高的
teacher	tutor	老师
technique	method	方法
test a new theory	try out his idea	验证观点
the arrival of farming	the introduction of agriculture	农业的引进
the lack of	have no access to	缺少
the premiere	perform for the first time	首映
the public	ordinary people	大众；普通人
thief	stealing	偷
threat	danger	威胁；危险
three consecutive days starting on Monday	Mon., Tue. & Wed.	从周一开始三个连续的早晨；周一，周二和周三
tolerant	put up with	忍受
too slow making up his mind	unsure	拿不定主意；不确定
top performers	leading musicians	顶级表演者；一流音乐家
trends or regularities	patterns	模式
turn into	transform into	变成；转化成
twice	double	双倍
typical	representative	有代表性的
uncommon/unusual	special	特别的

题目词汇	原文词汇	解释
under	below	在…下面
unhelpful	uncooperative	帮不上忙的；不合作的
unimportant	insignificant	不重要的
unrestricted	no legal limit	不受限制的
unsafe	dangerous	不安全的；危险的
up to	maximum	高达…；最高的
use	cultivate	种植
used	deployed/utilized	用于
useless and debatable	unreliable	不可靠的
value	see the need of	重视
vegetarian	people who don't eat meat or fish	素食主义者
very	extremely	极度
view/viewpoint	perspective	观点
wash off	rinse off	洗掉
water shortage	drought	缺水；干旱
waterways	rivers	水路；河流
ways	solutions	解决方法
wealth	fortune	财富
well designed	good planning	优秀的设计
well-known	prominent/be heard of/ famous	著名的

题目词汇	原文词汇	解释
where ... live	habitats	栖息地
wild animals	wildlife	野生动物
win	come first in the championship	赢得比赛
without	lack of	没有；缺乏

IELTS

Listening

雅思听力
真题词汇精讲

宋鹏昊　齐小霞　编著

练习册

浙江教育出版社·杭州

图书在版编目(CIP)数据

雅思听力真题词汇精讲 / 宋鹏昊，齐小霞编著. --
杭州 ：浙江教育出版社，2022.5
ISBN 978-7-5722-3325-8

Ⅰ. ①雅… Ⅱ. ①宋… ②齐… Ⅲ. ①IELTS－词汇－
自学参考资料 Ⅳ. ①H313

中国版本图书馆CIP数据核字(2022)第056800号

雅思听力真题词汇精讲
YASI TINGLI ZHENTI CIHUI JING JIANG
宋鹏昊 齐小霞 编著

责任编辑	赵清刚
美术编辑	韩 波
责任校对	马立改
责任印务	时小娟
封面设计	李 倩
出版发行	浙江教育出版社
	地址：杭州市天目山路40号
	邮编：310013
	电话：（0571）85170300－80928
	邮箱：dywh@xdf.cn
印　刷	三河市百盛印装有限公司
开　本	710mm×1000mm　1/16
成品尺寸	168mm×240mm
印　张	18.25
字　数	225 000
版　次	2022年5月第1版
印　次	2022年5月第1次印刷
标准书号	ISBN 978-7-5722-3325-8
定　价	45.00元（全两册）

目录

01
CHAPTER

雅思听力真题
考点词

本章音频

第一节 基础考点

一 纯数字

听录音，写出听到的数字。

Exercise 1

题号	数字
1	
2	
3	
4	
5	
6	
7	
8	
9	
10	

Exercise 2

题号	数字
1	
2	
3	
4	
5	
6	
7	
8	
9	
10	

Exercise 3

题号	数字
1	
2	
3	
4	

Exercise 4

题号	数字
1	
2	
3	
4	

题号	数字
5	
6	
7	
8	
9	
10	

题号	数字
5	
6	
7	
8	
9	
10	

二 长数字

听录音，写出听到的数字。

Exercise 1

题号	数字
1	
2	
3	
4	
5	
6	
7	
8	
9	
10	

Exercise 2

题号	数字
1	
2	
3	
4	
5	
6	
7	
8	
9	
10	

Exercise 3

题号	数字
1	
2	
3	
4	
5	

题号	数字
6	
7	
8	
9	
10	

三 字母与数字

听录音，写出听到的信息。

Exercise 1

题号	听到的信息
1	
2	
3	
4	
5	
6	
7	
8	
9	
10	

Exercise 2

题号	听到的信息
1	
2	
3	
4	
5	
6	
7	
8	
9	
10	

Exercise 3

题号	听到的信息
1	
2	
3	
4	
5	

题号	听到的信息
6	
7	
8	
9	
10	

四　单位

听录音，写出听到的信息。

Exercise 1

题号	听到的信息
1	
2	
3	
4	
5	
6	
7	
8	
9	
10	

Exercise 2

题号	听到的信息
1	
2	
3	
4	
5	
6	
7	
8	
9	
10	

五 地址

听录音，写出听到的地址。

Exercise 1

题号	地址
1	
2	
3	
4	
5	
6	
7	
8	
9	
10	

Exercise 2

题号	地址
1	
2	
3	
4	
5	
6	
7	
8	
9	
10	

Exercise 3

题号	地址
1	
2	
3	
4	
5	

题号	地址
6	
7	
8	
9	
10	

六 日期

听录音，写出听到的日期。

Exercise 1

题号	日期
1	
2	
3	
4	
5	
6	
7	
8	
9	
10	

Exercise 2

题号	日期
1	
2	
3	
4	
5	
6	
7	
8	
9	
10	

Exercise 3

题号	日期
1	
2	
3	
4	
5	

题号	日期
6	
7	
8	
9	
10	

七 时间

听录音，写出听到的时间。

Exercise 1

题号	时间
1	
2	
3	
4	
5	
6	
7	
8	
9	
10	

Exercise 2

题号	时间
1	
2	
3	
4	
5	
6	
7	
8	
9	
10	

Exercise 3

题号	时间
1	
2	
3	
4	
5	

题号	时间
6	
7	
8	
9	
10	

一　多音词

听录音，写出听到的单词，并写出其词性和释义。

Exercise 1

题号	单词	词性及释义
1		
2		
3		
4		
5		
6		
7		
8		
9		
10		

Exercise 2

题号	单词	词性及释义
1		
2		
3		
4		
5		
6		
7		
8		
9		
10		

二　同音异形词

听录音，写出听到的单词，每题写出 2 个单词。

Exercise 1

题号	单词	单词
1		
2		

Exercise 2

题号	单词	单词
1		
2		

题号	单词	单词
3		
4		
5		
6		
7		
8		
9		
10		

题号	单词	单词
3		
4		
5		
6		
7		
8		
9		
10		

三 发音相近词

听录音，写出听到的单词。

Exercise 1

题号	单词
1	
2	
3	
4	
5	
6	
7	
8	
9	
10	

Exercise 2

题号	单词
1	
2	
3	
4	
5	
6	
7	
8	
9	
10	

Exercise 3

题号	单词
1	
2	
3	
4	
5	
6	
7	
8	
9	
10	

Exercise 4

题号	单词
1	
2	
3	
4	
5	
6	
7	
8	
9	
10	

Exercise 5

题号	单词
1	
2	
3	
4	
5	
6	
7	
8	
9	
10	

Exercise 6

题号	单词
1	
2	
3	
4	
5	
6	
7	
8	
9	
10	

Exercise **7**

题号	单词
1	
2	
3	
4	
5	
6	
7	
8	
9	
10	

Exercise **8**

题号	单词
1	
2	
3	
4	
5	
6	
7	
8	
9	
10	

Exercise **9**

题号	单词
1	
2	
3	
4	
5	
6	
7	
8	
9	
10	

Exercise **10**

题号	单词
1	
2	
3	
4	
5	
6	
7	
8	
9	
10	

（四）英、美式拼写

听录音，写出听到的单词的英式拼写与美式拼写。

Exercise 1

题号	英式拼写	美式拼写
1		
2		
3		
4		
5		
6		
7		
8		
9		
10		

Exercise 2

题号	英式拼写	美式拼写
1		
2		
3		
4		
5		
6		
7		
8		
9		
10		

Exercise 3

题号	英式拼写	美式拼写
1		
2		
3		
4		
5		

题号	英式拼写	美式拼写
6		
7		
8		
9		
10		

五 连字符

听录音，写出听到的单词。

Exercise 1

题号	单词
1	
2	
3	
4	
5	
6	
7	
8	
9	
10	

Exercise 2

题号	单词
1	
2	
3	
4	
5	
6	
7	
8	
9	
10	

六 缩写

写出以下缩写所代表的完整表达。

Exercise 1

题号	缩写	完整表达
1	EU	
2	ATM	
3	CV	
4	NB	
5	p.m.	

Exercise 2

题号	缩写	完整表达
1	PDF	
2	a.m.	
3	WTO	
4	UFO	
5	POS	

题号	缩写	完整表达
6	IT	
7	CPU	
8	APEC	
9	CEO	
10	UPS	

题号	缩写	完整表达
6	BC	
7	BBQ	
8	IQ	
9	UNESCO	
10	GPS	

第三节　高频考点词

 名词

听录音，写出听到的单词。

Exercise 1

题号	单词
1	
2	
3	
4	
5	
6	
7	
8	
9	
10	

Exercise 2

题号	单词
1	
2	
3	
4	
5	
6	
7	
8	
9	
10	

Exercise 3

题号	单词
1	
2	
3	
4	
5	
6	
7	
8	
9	
10	

Exercise 4

题号	单词
1	
2	
3	
4	
5	
6	
7	
8	
9	
10	

Exercise 5

题号	单词
1	
2	
3	
4	
5	
6	
7	
8	
9	
10	

Exercise 6

题号	单词
1	
2	
3	
4	
5	
6	
7	
8	
9	
10	

Exercise 7

题号	单词
1	
2	
3	
4	
5	
6	
7	
8	
9	
10	

Exercise 8

题号	单词
1	
2	
3	
4	
5	
6	
7	
8	
9	
10	

Exercise 9

题号	单词
1	
2	
3	
4	
5	
6	
7	
8	
9	
10	

Exercise 10

题号	单词
1	
2	
3	
4	
5	
6	
7	
8	
9	
10	

Exercise 11

题号	单词
1	
2	
3	
4	
5	
6	
7	
8	
9	
10	

Exercise 12

题号	单词
1	
2	
3	
4	
5	
6	
7	
8	
9	
10	

Exercise 13

题号	单词
1	
2	
3	
4	
5	
6	
7	
8	
9	
10	

Exercise 14

题号	单词
1	
2	
3	
4	
5	
6	
7	
8	
9	
10	

Exercise 15

题号	单词
1	
2	
3	
4	
5	
6	
7	
8	
9	
10	

Exercise 16

题号	单词
1	
2	
3	
4	
5	
6	
7	
8	
9	
10	

Exercise 17

题号	单词
1	
2	
3	
4	
5	
6	
7	
8	
9	
10	

Exercise 18

题号	单词
1	
2	
3	
4	
5	
6	
7	
8	
9	
10	

Exercise 19

题号	单词
1	
2	
3	
4	
5	
6	
7	
8	
9	
10	

Exercise 20

题号	单词
1	
2	
3	
4	
5	
6	
7	
8	
9	
10	

Exercise 21

题号	单词
1	
2	
3	
4	
5	
6	
7	
8	
9	
10	

Exercise 22

题号	单词
1	
2	
3	
4	
5	
6	
7	
8	
9	
10	

Exercise 23

题号	单词
1	
2	
3	
4	
5	
6	
7	
8	
9	
10	

Exercise 24

题号	单词
1	
2	
3	
4	
5	
6	
7	
8	
9	
10	

Exercise 25

题号	单词
1	
2	
3	
4	
5	
6	
7	
8	
9	
10	

Exercise 26

题号	单词
1	
2	
3	
4	
5	
6	
7	
8	
9	
10	

Exercise 27

题号	单词
1	
2	
3	
4	
5	
6	
7	
8	
9	
10	

Exercise 28

题号	单词
1	
2	
3	
4	
5	
6	
7	
8	
9	
10	

Exercise 29

题号	单词
1	
2	
3	
4	
5	
6	
7	
8	
9	
10	

Exercise 30

题号	单词
1	
2	
3	
4	
5	
6	
7	
8	
9	
10	

Exercise 31

题号	单词
1	
2	
3	
4	
5	
6	
7	
8	
9	
10	

Exercise 32

题号	单词
1	
2	
3	
4	
5	
6	
7	
8	
9	
10	

Exercise 33

题号	单词
1	
2	
3	
4	
5	
6	
7	
8	
9	
10	

Exercise 34

题号	单词
1	
2	
3	
4	
5	
6	
7	
8	
9	
10	

Exercise 35

题号	单词
1	
2	
3	
4	
5	
6	
7	
8	
9	
10	

Exercise 36

题号	单词
1	
2	
3	
4	
5	
6	
7	
8	
9	
10	

Exercise 37

题号	单词
1	
2	
3	
4	
5	
6	
7	
8	
9	
10	

Exercise 38

题号	单词
1	
2	
3	
4	
5	
6	
7	
8	
9	
10	

Exercise 39

题号	单词
1	
2	
3	
4	
5	
6	
7	
8	
9	
10	

Exercise 40

题号	单词
1	
2	
3	
4	
5	
6	
7	
8	
9	
10	

Exercise 41

题号	单词
1	
2	
3	
4	
5	
6	
7	
8	
9	
10	

Exercise 42

题号	单词
1	
2	
3	
4	
5	
6	
7	
8	
9	
10	

Exercise 43

题号	单词
1	
2	
3	
4	
5	
6	
7	
8	
9	
10	

Exercise 44

题号	单词
1	
2	
3	
4	
5	
6	
7	
8	
9	
10	

Exercise 45

题号	单词
1	
2	
3	
4	
5	
6	
7	
8	
9	
10	

Exercise 46

题号	单词
1	
2	
3	
4	
5	
6	
7	
8	
9	
10	

Exercise 47

题号	单词
1	
2	
3	
4	
5	
6	
7	
8	
9	
10	

Exercise 48

题号	单词
1	
2	
3	
4	
5	
6	
7	
8	
9	
10	

Exercise 49

题号	单词
1	
2	
3	
4	
5	
6	
7	
8	
9	
10	

Exercise 50

题号	单词
1	
2	
3	
4	
5	
6	
7	
8	
9	
10	

Exercise 51

题号	单词
1	
2	
3	
4	
5	
6	
7	
8	
9	
10	

Exercise 52

题号	单词
1	
2	
3	
4	
5	
6	
7	
8	
9	
10	

Exercise 53

题号	单词
1	
2	
3	
4	
5	
6	
7	
8	
9	
10	

Exercise 54

题号	单词
1	
2	
3	
4	
5	
6	
7	
8	
9	
10	

Exercise 55

题号	单词
1	
2	
3	
4	
5	
6	
7	
8	
9	
10	

Exercise 56

题号	单词
1	
2	
3	
4	
5	
6	
7	
8	
9	
10	

Exercise 57

题号	单词
1	
2	
3	
4	
5	
6	
7	
8	
9	
10	

Exercise 58

题号	单词
1	
2	
3	
4	
5	
6	
7	
8	
9	
10	

Exercise 59

题号	单词
1	
2	
3	
4	
5	
6	
7	
8	
9	
10	

Exercise 60

题号	单词
1	
2	
3	
4	
5	
6	
7	
8	
9	
10	

Exercise 61

题号	单词
1	
2	
3	
4	
5	
6	
7	
8	
9	
10	

Exercise 62

题号	单词
1	
2	
3	
4	
5	
6	
7	
8	
9	
10	

Exercise 63

题号	单词
1	
2	
3	
4	
5	
6	
7	
8	
9	
10	

Exercise 64

题号	单词
1	
2	
3	
4	
5	
6	
7	
8	
9	
10	

Exercise 65

题号	单词
1	
2	
3	
4	
5	
6	
7	
8	
9	
10	

Exercise 66

题号	单词
1	
2	
3	
4	
5	
6	
7	
8	
9	
10	

Exercise 67

题号	单词
1	
2	
3	
4	
5	
6	
7	
8	
9	
10	

Exercise 68

题号	单词
1	
2	
3	
4	
5	
6	
7	
8	
9	
10	

Exercise 69

题号	单词
1	
2	
3	
4	
5	
6	
7	
8	
9	
10	

Exercise 70

题号	单词
1	
2	
3	
4	
5	
6	
7	
8	
9	
10	

Exercise 71

题号	单词
1	
2	
3	
4	
5	
6	
7	
8	
9	
10	

Exercise 72

题号	单词
1	
2	
3	
4	
5	
6	
7	
8	
9	
10	

Exercise 73

题号	单词
1	
2	
3	
4	
5	
6	
7	
8	
9	
10	

Exercise 74

题号	单词
1	
2	
3	
4	
5	
6	
7	
8	
9	
10	

Exercise 75

题号	单词
1	
2	
3	
4	
5	
6	
7	
8	
9	
10	

Exercise 76

题号	单词
1	
2	
3	
4	
5	
6	
7	
8	
9	
10	

Exercise 77

题号	单词
1	
2	
3	
4	
5	
6	
7	
8	
9	
10	

Exercise 78

题号	单词
1	
2	
3	
4	
5	
6	
7	
8	
9	
10	

Exercise 79

题号	单词
1	
2	
3	
4	
5	
6	
7	
8	
9	
10	

Exercise 80

题号	单词
1	
2	
3	
4	
5	
6	
7	
8	
9	
10	

Exercise 81

题号	单词
1	
2	
3	
4	
5	
6	
7	
8	
9	
10	

Exercise 82

题号	单词
1	
2	
3	
4	
5	
6	
7	
8	
9	
10	

Exercise 83

题号	单词
1	
2	
3	
4	
5	
6	
7	
8	
9	
10	

Exercise 84

题号	单词
1	
2	
3	
4	
5	
6	
7	
8	
9	
10	

Exercise 85

题号	单词
1	
2	
3	
4	
5	
6	
7	
8	
9	
10	

Exercise 86

题号	单词
1	
2	
3	
4	
5	
6	
7	
8	
9	
10	

Exercise 87

题号	单词
1	
2	
3	
4	
5	
6	
7	
8	
9	
10	

Exercise 88

题号	单词
1	
2	
3	
4	
5	
6	
7	
8	
9	
10	

Exercise 89

题号	单词
1	
2	
3	
4	
5	
6	
7	
8	
9	
10	

Exercise 90

题号	单词
1	
2	
3	
4	
5	
6	
7	
8	
9	
10	

Exercise 91

题号	单词
1	
2	
3	
4	
5	
6	
7	
8	
9	
10	

Exercise 92

题号	单词
1	
2	
3	
4	
5	
6	
7	
8	
9	
10	

Exercise 93

题号	单词
1	
2	
3	
4	
5	
6	
7	
8	
9	
10	

Exercise 94

题号	单词
1	
2	
3	
4	
5	
6	
7	
8	
9	
10	

Exercise 95

题号	单词
1	
2	
3	
4	
5	
6	
7	
8	
9	
10	

Exercise 96

题号	单词
1	
2	
3	
4	
5	
6	
7	
8	
9	
10	

Exercise 97

题号	单词
1	
2	
3	
4	
5	
6	
7	
8	
9	
10	

Exercise 98

题号	单词
1	
2	
3	
4	
5	
6	
7	
8	
9	
10	

Exercise 99

题号	单词
1	
2	
3	
4	
5	
6	
7	
8	
9	
10	

Exercise 100

题号	单词
1	
2	
3	
4	
5	
6	
7	
8	
9	
10	

二 动词

听录音，写出听到的单词。

Exercise 1

题号	单词
1	
2	
3	
4	
5	
6	
7	

Exercise 2

题号	单词
1	
2	
3	
4	
5	
6	
7	

题号	单词
8	
9	
10	

题号	单词
8	
9	
10	

Exercise 3

题号	单词
1	
2	
3	
4	
5	
6	
7	
8	
9	
10	

Exercise 4

题号	单词
1	
2	
3	
4	
5	
6	
7	
8	
9	
10	

Exercise 5

题号	单词
1	
2	
3	
4	

Exercise 6

题号	单词
1	
2	
3	
4	

题号	单词
5	
6	
7	
8	
9	
10	

题号	单词
5	
6	
7	
8	
9	
10	

Exercise 7

题号	单词
1	
2	
3	
4	
5	
6	
7	
8	
9	
10	

Exercise 8

题号	单词
1	
2	
3	
4	
5	
6	
7	
8	
9	
10	

Exercise 9

题号	单词
1	

Exercise 10

题号	单词
1	

题号	单词
2	
3	
4	
5	
6	
7	
8	
9	
10	

题号	单词
2	
3	
4	
5	
6	
7	
8	
9	
10	

Exercise 11

题号	单词
1	
2	
3	
4	
5	
6	
7	
8	
9	
10	

Exercise 12

题号	单词
1	
2	
3	
4	
5	
6	
7	
8	
9	
10	

Exercise 13

题号	单词
1	
2	
3	
4	
5	
6	
7	
8	
9	
10	

Exercise 14

题号	单词
1	
2	
3	
4	
5	
6	
7	
8	
9	
10	

Exercise 15

题号	单词
1	
2	
3	
4	
5	

题号	单词
6	
7	
8	
9	
10	

三　形容词

听录音，写出听到的单词。

Exercise 1

题号	单词
1	
2	
3	
4	
5	
6	
7	
8	
9	
10	

Exercise 2

题号	单词
1	
2	
3	
4	
5	
6	
7	
8	
9	
10	

Exercise 3

题号	单词
1	
2	
3	
4	
5	
6	
7	

Exercise 4

题号	单词
1	
2	
3	
4	
5	
6	
7	

题号	单词
8	
9	
10	

题号	单词
8	
9	
10	

Exercise 5

题号	单词
1	
2	
3	
4	
5	
6	
7	
8	
9	
10	

Exercise 6

题号	单词
1	
2	
3	
4	
5	
6	
7	
8	
9	
10	

Exercise 7

题号	单词
1	
2	
3	
4	

Exercise 8

题号	单词
1	
2	
3	
4	

题号	单词
5	
6	
7	
8	
9	
10	

题号	单词
5	
6	
7	
8	
9	
10	

Exercise 9

题号	单词
1	
2	
3	
4	
5	
6	
7	
8	
9	
10	

Exercise 10

题号	单词
1	
2	
3	
4	
5	
6	
7	
8	
9	
10	

Exercise 11

题号	单词
1	

Exercise 12

题号	单词
1	

题号	单词		题号	单词
2			2	
3			3	
4			4	
5			5	
6			6	
7			7	
8			8	
9			9	
10			10	

Exercise 13

Exercise 14

题号	单词		题号	单词
1			1	
2			2	
3			3	
4			4	
5			5	
6			6	
7			7	
8			8	
9			9	
10			10	

Exercise 15

题号	单词
1	
2	
3	
4	
5	
6	
7	
8	
9	
10	

Exercise 16

题号	单词
1	
2	
3	
4	
5	
6	
7	
8	
9	
10	

Exercise 17

题号	单词
1	
2	
3	
4	
5	
6	
7	
8	
9	
10	

Exercise 18

题号	单词
1	
2	
3	
4	
5	
6	
7	
8	
9	
10	

Exercise 19

题号	单词
1	
2	
3	
4	
5	
6	
7	
8	
9	
10	

Exercise 20

题号	单词
1	
2	
3	
4	
5	
6	
7	
8	
9	
10	

Exercise 21

题号	单词
1	
2	
3	
4	
5	
6	
7	
8	
9	
10	

Exercise 22

题号	单词
1	
2	
3	
4	
5	
6	
7	
8	
9	
10	

Exercise 23

题号	单词
1	
2	
3	
4	
5	
6	
7	
8	
9	
10	

Exercise 24

题号	单词
1	
2	
3	
4	
5	
6	
7	
8	
9	
10	

Exercise 25

题号	单词
1	
2	
3	
4	
5	

题号	单词
6	
7	
8	
9	
10	

四　副词

听录音，写出听到的单词。

Exercise 1

题号	单词
1	
2	
3	
4	
5	
6	
7	
8	
9	
10	

Exercise 2

题号	单词
1	
2	
3	
4	
5	
6	
7	
8	
9	
10	

Exercise 3

题号	单词
1	
2	
3	
4	
5	
6	
7	

Exercise 4

题号	单词
1	
2	
3	
4	
5	
6	
7	

题号	单词
8	
9	
10	

题号	单词
8	
9	
10	

五 常考搭配

听录音，写出听到的搭配。

Exercise 1

题号	搭配
1	
2	
3	
4	
5	
6	
7	
8	
9	
10	

Exercise 2

题号	搭配
1	
2	
3	
4	
5	
6	
7	
8	
9	
10	

Exercise 3

题号	搭配
1	
2	

Exercise 4

题号	搭配
1	
2	

题号	搭配
3	
4	
5	
6	
7	
8	
9	
10	

题号	搭配
3	
4	
5	
6	
7	
8	
9	
10	

Exercise 5

题号	搭配
1	
2	
3	
4	
5	
6	
7	
8	
9	
10	

Exercise 6

题号	搭配
1	
2	
3	
4	
5	
6	
7	
8	
9	
10	

Exercise 7

题号	搭配
1	
2	
3	
4	
5	
6	
7	
8	
9	
10	

Exercise 8

题号	搭配
1	
2	
3	
4	
5	
6	
7	
8	
9	
10	

六 地名及相关词汇

听录音，写出听到的地名及相关词汇。

Exercise 1

题号	单词
1	
2	
3	
4	
5	
6	
7	

Exercise 2

题号	单词
1	
2	
3	
4	
5	
6	
7	

题号	单词
8	
9	
10	

题号	单词
8	
9	
10	

Exercise 3

题号	单词
1	
2	
3	
4	
5	
6	
7	
8	
9	
10	

Exercise 4

题号	单词
1	
2	
3	
4	
5	
6	
7	
8	
9	
10	

Exercise 5

题号	单词
1	
2	
3	
4	
5	

题号	单词
6	
7	
8	
9	
10	

02
CHAPTER

雅思听力
场景词汇

本章音频

第一节　住宿（Accommodation）

听录音，写出听到的场景词汇。

Exercise 1

题号	场景词汇
1	
2	
3	
4	
5	
6	
7	
8	
9	
10	

Exercise 2

题号	场景词汇
1	
2	
3	
4	
5	
6	
7	
8	
9	
10	

Exercise 3

题号	场景词汇
1	
2	
3	
4	
5	

Exercise 4

题号	场景词汇
1	
2	
3	
4	
5	

题号	场景词汇
6	
7	
8	
9	
10	

题号	场景词汇
6	
7	
8	
9	
10	

Exercise 5

题号	场景词汇
1	
2	
3	
4	
5	
6	
7	
8	
9	
10	

Exercise 6

题号	场景词汇
1	
2	
3	
4	
5	
6	
7	
8	
9	
10	

Exercise 7

题号	场景词汇
1	
2	

Exercise 8

题号	场景词汇
1	
2	

题号	场景词汇
3	
4	
5	
6	
7	
8	
9	
10	

题号	场景词汇
3	
4	
5	
6	
7	
8	
9	
10	

Exercise 9

题号	场景词汇
1	
2	
3	
4	
5	
6	
7	
8	
9	
10	

Exercise 10

题号	场景词汇
1	
2	
3	
4	
5	
6	
7	
8	
9	
10	

听录音，写出听到的场景词汇。

Exercise 1

题号	场景词汇
1	
2	
3	
4	
5	
6	
7	
8	
9	
10	

Exercise 2

题号	场景词汇
1	
2	
3	
4	
5	
6	
7	
8	
9	
10	

Exercise 3

题号	场景词汇
1	
2	
3	
4	
5	

Exercise 4

题号	场景词汇
1	
2	
3	
4	
5	

题号	场景词汇
6	
7	
8	
9	
10	

题号	场景词汇
6	
7	
8	
9	
10	

Exercise 5

题号	场景词汇
1	
2	
3	
4	
5	
6	
7	
8	
9	
10	

Exercise 6

题号	场景词汇
1	
2	
3	
4	
5	
6	
7	
8	
9	
10	

Exercise 7

题号	场景词汇
1	
2	

Exercise 8

题号	场景词汇
1	
2	

题号	场景词汇
3	
4	
5	
6	
7	
8	
9	
10	

题号	场景词汇
3	
4	
5	
6	
7	
8	
9	
10	

第三节　旅游（Travel）

听录音，写出听到的场景词汇。

Exercise 1

题号	场景词汇
1	
2	
3	
4	
5	
6	
7	

Exercise 2

题号	场景词汇
1	
2	
3	
4	
5	
6	
7	

题号	场景词汇
8	
9	
10	

题号	场景词汇
8	
9	
10	

Exercise 3

题号	场景词汇
1	
2	
3	
4	
5	
6	
7	
8	
9	
10	

Exercise 4

题号	场景词汇
1	
2	
3	
4	
5	
6	
7	
8	
9	
10	

Exercise 5

题号	场景词汇
1	
2	
3	
4	

Exercise 6

题号	场景词汇
1	
2	
3	
4	

题号	场景词汇
5	
6	
7	
8	
9	
10	

题号	场景词汇
5	
6	
7	
8	
9	
10	

Exercise 7

题号	场景词汇
1	
2	
3	
4	
5	
6	
7	
8	
9	
10	

Exercise 8

题号	场景词汇
1	
2	
3	
4	
5	
6	
7	
8	
9	
10	

Exercise 9

题号	场景词汇
1	

Exercise 10

题号	场景词汇
1	

题号	场景词汇
2	
3	
4	
5	
6	
7	
8	
9	
10	

题号	场景词汇
2	
3	
4	
5	
6	
7	
8	
9	
10	

Exercise 11

题号	场景词汇
1	
2	
3	
4	
5	
6	
7	
8	
9	
10	

Exercise 12

题号	场景词汇
1	
2	
3	
4	
5	
6	
7	
8	
9	
10	

Exercise 13

题号	场景词汇
1	
2	
3	
4	
5	
6	
7	
8	
9	
10	

Exercise 14

题号	场景词汇
1	
2	
3	
4	
5	
6	
7	
8	
9	
10	

Exercise 15

题号	场景词汇
1	
2	
3	
4	
5	
6	
7	
8	
9	
10	

Exercise 16

题号	场景词汇
1	
2	
3	
4	
5	
6	
7	
8	
9	
10	

Exercise 17

题号	场景词汇
1	
2	
3	
4	
5	
6	
7	
8	
9	
10	

Exercise 18

题号	场景词汇
1	
2	
3	
4	
5	
6	
7	
8	
9	
10	

Exercise 19

题号	场景词汇
1	
2	
3	
4	
5	
6	
7	
8	
9	
10	

Exercise 20

题号	场景词汇
1	
2	
3	
4	
5	
6	
7	
8	
9	
10	

听录音，写出听到的场景词汇。

Exercise 1

题号	场景词汇
1	
2	
3	
4	
5	
6	
7	
8	
9	
10	

Exercise 2

题号	场景词汇
1	
2	
3	
4	
5	
6	
7	
8	
9	
10	

Exercise 3

题号	场景词汇
1	
2	
3	
4	
5	

Exercise 4

题号	场景词汇
1	
2	
3	
4	
5	

题号	场景词汇
6	
7	
8	
9	
10	

题号	场景词汇
6	
7	
8	
9	
10	

Exercise 5

题号	场景词汇
1	
2	
3	
4	
5	
6	
7	
8	
9	
10	

Exercise 6

题号	场景词汇
1	
2	
3	
4	
5	
6	
7	
8	
9	
10	

Exercise 7

题号	场景词汇
1	
2	

Exercise 8

题号	场景词汇
1	
2	

题号	场景词汇
3	
4	
5	
6	
7	
8	
9	
10	

题号	场景词汇
3	
4	
5	
6	
7	
8	
9	
10	

第五节　社会生活（Social Life）

听录音，写出听到的场景词汇。

Exercise 1

题号	场景词汇
1	
2	
3	
4	
5	
6	
7	

Exercise 2

题号	场景词汇
1	
2	
3	
4	
5	
6	
7	

题号	场景词汇
8	
9	
10	

题号	场景词汇
8	
9	
10	

Exercise 3

题号	场景词汇
1	
2	
3	
4	
5	
6	
7	
8	
9	
10	

Exercise 4

题号	场景词汇
1	
2	
3	
4	
5	
6	
7	
8	
9	
10	

Exercise 5

题号	场景词汇
1	
2	
3	
4	

Exercise 6

题号	场景词汇
1	
2	
3	
4	

题号	场景词汇
5	
6	
7	
8	
9	
10	

题号	场景词汇
5	
6	
7	
8	
9	
10	

Exercise 7

题号	场景词汇
1	
2	
3	
4	
5	
6	
7	
8	
9	
10	

Exercise 8

题号	场景词汇
1	
2	
3	
4	
5	
6	
7	
8	
9	
10	

Exercise 9

题号	场景词汇
1	

Exercise 10

题号	场景词汇
1	

题号	场景词汇		题号	场景词汇
2			2	
3			3	
4			4	
5			5	
6			6	
7			7	
8			8	
9			9	
10			10	

第六节　工作（Work）

听录音，写出听到的场景词汇。

Exercise 1

题号	场景词汇
1	
2	
3	
4	
5	

Exercise 2

题号	场景词汇
1	
2	
3	
4	
5	

题号	场景词汇
6	
7	
8	
9	
10	

题号	场景词汇
6	
7	
8	
9	
10	

Exercise 3

题号	场景词汇
1	
2	
3	
4	
5	
6	
7	
8	
9	
10	

Exercise 4

题号	场景词汇
1	
2	
3	
4	
5	
6	
7	
8	
9	
10	

Exercise 5

题号	场景词汇
1	
2	

Exercise 6

题号	场景词汇
1	
2	

题号	场景词汇
3	
4	
5	
6	
7	
8	
9	
10	

题号	场景词汇
3	
4	
5	
6	
7	
8	
9	
10	

Exercise 7

题号	场景词汇
1	
2	
3	
4	
5	
6	
7	
8	
9	
10	

Exercise 8

题号	场景词汇
1	
2	
3	
4	
5	
6	
7	
8	
9	
10	

听录音，写出听到的场景词汇。

Exercise 1

题号	场景词汇
1	
2	
3	
4	
5	
6	
7	
8	
9	
10	

Exercise 2

题号	场景词汇
1	
2	
3	
4	
5	
6	
7	
8	
9	
10	

Exercise 3

题号	场景词汇
1	
2	
3	
4	
5	

Exercise 4

题号	场景词汇
1	
2	
3	
4	
5	

题号	场景词汇
6	
7	
8	
9	
10	

题号	场景词汇
6	
7	
8	
9	
10	

Exercise 5

题号	场景词汇
1	
2	
3	
4	
5	
6	
7	
8	
9	
10	

Exercise 6

题号	场景词汇
1	
2	
3	
4	
5	
6	
7	
8	
9	
10	

Exercise 7

题号	场景词汇
1	
2	

Exercise 8

题号	场景词汇
1	
2	

题号	场景词汇
3	
4	
5	
6	
7	
8	
9	
10	

题号	场景词汇
3	
4	
5	
6	
7	
8	
9	
10	

Exercise 9

题号	场景词汇
1	
2	
3	
4	
5	
6	
7	
8	
9	
10	

Exercise 10

题号	场景词汇
1	
2	
3	
4	
5	
6	
7	
8	
9	
10	

Exercise 11

题号	场景词汇
1	
2	
3	
4	
5	
6	
7	
8	
9	
10	

Exercise 12

题号	场景词汇
1	
2	
3	
4	
5	
6	
7	
8	
9	
10	

Exercise 13

题号	场景词汇
1	
2	
3	
4	
5	
6	
7	
8	
9	
10	

Exercise 14

题号	场景词汇
1	
2	
3	
4	
5	
6	
7	
8	
9	
10	

Exercise 15

题号	场景词汇		题号	场景词汇
1			6	
2			7	
3			8	
4			9	
5			10	

第八节　讲座（Lecture）

听录音，写出听到的场景词汇。

Exercise 1

题号	场景词汇
1	
2	
3	
4	
5	
6	
7	
8	
9	
10	

Exercise 2

题号	场景词汇
1	
2	
3	
4	
5	
6	
7	
8	
9	
10	

Exercise 3

题号	场景词汇
1	
2	
3	
4	
5	
6	
7	
8	
9	
10	

Exercise 4

题号	场景词汇
1	
2	
3	
4	
5	
6	
7	
8	
9	
10	

Exercise 5

题号	场景词汇
1	
2	
3	
4	
5	
6	
7	
8	
9	
10	

Exercise 6

题号	场景词汇
1	
2	
3	
4	
5	
6	
7	
8	
9	
10	

Exercise 7

题号	场景词汇
1	
2	
3	
4	
5	
6	
7	
8	
9	
10	

Exercise 8

题号	场景词汇
1	
2	
3	
4	
5	
6	
7	
8	
9	
10	

Exercise 9

题号	场景词汇
1	
2	
3	
4	
5	
6	
7	
8	
9	
10	

Exercise 10

题号	场景词汇
1	
2	
3	
4	
5	
6	
7	
8	
9	
10	

Exercise 11

题号	场景词汇
1	
2	
3	
4	
5	
6	
7	
8	
9	
10	

Exercise 12

题号	场景词汇
1	
2	
3	
4	
5	
6	
7	
8	
9	
10	

Exercise 13

题号	场景词汇
1	
2	
3	
4	
5	
6	
7	
8	
9	
10	

Exercise 14

题号	场景词汇
1	
2	
3	
4	
5	
6	
7	
8	
9	
10	

Exercise 15

题号	场景词汇
1	
2	
3	
4	
5	

题号	场景词汇
6	
7	
8	
9	
10	

03
CHAPTER

听力同义
替换词表

本章音频

你将在录音中听到五个单词或词组，请将听到的单词或词组与下面题目中含义一致的单词或词组连线。

Exercise 1

题号	单词 / 词组
1	A. be knowledgeable about
2	B. make the arrangements
3	C. passion for/be keen on
4	D. skeleton
5	E. references

Exercise 2

题号	单词 / 词组
1	A. official
2	B. disturbing
3	C. be put on hold
4	D. return
5	E. at least

Exercise 3

题号	单词 / 词组
1	A. quantities
2	B. back/at the back of
3	C. overheads
4	D. get started
5	E. being an apprentice

Exercise 4

题号	单词 / 词组
1	A. check with someone
2	B. in the long-term future
3	C. get mixed up
4	D. accessible to the ordinary people
5	E. economical

Exercise 5

题号	单词／词组
1	A. make it wider
2	B. field
3	C. improve their sales figures
4	D. target at
5	E. about

Exercise 6

题号	单词／词组
1	A. strengthen
2	B. superior
3	C. alternative
4	D. change
5	E. a few

第二节　字母 C

你将在录音中听到五个单词或词组，请将听到的单词或词组与下面题目中含义一致的单词或词组连线。

Exercise 1

题号	单词／词组
1	A. rural areas
2	B. amend
3	C. expensive
4	D. cargoes
5	E. keep in touch with

Exercise 2

题号	单词／词组
1	A. results
2	B. ambiguous
3	C. be on sale
4	D. revert to
5	E. babysitting

Exercise 3

题号	单词 / 词组
1	A. get in touch with
2	B. lead to
3	C. design
4	D. coincidence
5	E. at present

Exercise 4

题号	单词 / 词组
1	A. check with someone
2	B. make
3	C. global warming
4	D. cold
5	E. fees

Exercise 5

题号	单词 / 词组
1	A. proportion
2	B. tint
3	C. cities built by the sea
4	D. definitive
5	E. shifting

Exercise 6

题号	单词 / 词组
1	A. must
2	B. associated with
3	C. shorten
4	D. work together
5	E. enough

你将在录音中听到五个单词或词组，请将听到的单词或词组与下面题目中含义一致的单词或词组连线。

Exercise 1

题号	单词 / 词组
1	A. improve
2	B. available
3	C. go through
4	D. attach to
5	E. minority

Exercise 2

题号	单词 / 词组
1	A. a lot of energy
2	B. more quickly
3	C. above
4	D. complete
5	E. test

Exercise 3

题号	单词 / 词组
1	A. consult
2	B. reduced
3	C. rapid motion
4	D. talk about
5	E. at the beginning

Exercise 4

题号	单词 / 词组
1	A. drainage channels
2	B. precise
3	C. noisy
4	D. amusement
5	E. assumption

Exercise 5

题号	单词/词组
1	A. demonstration
2	B. vanish
3	C. cities built by the sea
4	D. drive under 20 kilometres
5	E. emphasize

Exercise 6

题号	单词/词组
1	A. no places left
2	B. from Monday to Friday
3	C. order
4	D. hold-up
5	E. set up

第四节 字母 G-I

你将在录音中听到五个单词或词组，请将听到的单词或词组与下面题目中含义一致的单词或词组连线。

Exercise 1

题号	单词/词组
1	A. develop
2	B. houses
3	C. too hot
4	D. shy
5	E. feet

Exercise 2

题号	单词/词组
1	A. look out at the river
2	B. a tremendous need
3	C. straight away
4	D. hurt
5	E. on a large scale

Exercise 3

题号	单词 / 词组
1	A. working
2	B. present
3	C. significant
4	D. hand out
5	E. limited

Exercise 4

题号	单词 / 词组
1	A. plant vegetables
2	B. very supportive
3	C. in the shape of a human
4	D. frighten or injure
5	E. altogether

Exercise 5

题号	单词 / 词组
1	A. disruption
2	B. expanding
3	C. draw correct conclusions
4	D. busy roads
5	E. not expensive

Exercise 6

题号	单词 / 词组
1	A. exert
2	B. points/theories
3	C. reduce emissions on air pollution
4	D. visualize
5	E. enhance

你将在录音中听到五个单词或词组，请将听到的单词或词组与下面题目中含义一致的单词或词组连线。

Exercise 1

题号	单词 / 词组
1	A. quieter
2	B. a lot of
3	C. over
4	D. update
5	E. precious stones

Exercise 2

题号	单词 / 词组
1	A. iron forge
2	B. stay at a safe distance
3	C. achievable
4	D. get the wrong idea
5	E. massive/significant

Exercise 3

题号	单词 / 词组
1	A. drink
2	B. cutlery
3	C. buried
4	D. not to be too precise
5	E. major global corporations

Exercise 4

题号	单词 / 词组
1	A. note key information
2	B. most
3	C. supervise
4	D. make
5	E. effective

Exercise 5

题号	单词 / 词组
1	A. considerable time
2	B. signs
3	C. latest
4	D. trust
5	E. keep

Exercise 6

题号	单词 / 词组
1	A. observe
2	B. production
3	C. constructed from
4	D. people living nearby
5	E. limited

第六节　字母 O-Q

你将在录音中听到五个单词或词组，请将听到的单词或词组与下面题目中含义一致的单词或词组连线。

Exercise 1

题号	单词
1	A. sociable
2	B. calling
3	C. employees
4	D. antique
5	E. specific

Exercise 2

题号	单词 / 词组
1	A. balance conflicting needs
2	B. be given
3	C. safeguard/save
4	D. not allowed
5	E. contaminants

Exercise 3

题号	单词
1	A. follow
2	B. outbreak
3	C. poor
4	D. vegetables
5	E. draw

Exercise 4

题号	单词 / 词组
1	A. possible danger
2	B. old-fashioned
3	C. stop participating
4	D. reduced
5	E. vulnerable physically

Exercise 5

题号	单词 / 词组
1	A. individual
2	B. young and old
3	C. put at the beginning
4	D. exterior
5	E. is scored for

Exercise 6

题号	单词 / 词组
1	A. preference
2	B. give
3	C. neighbours
4	D. job
5	E. not far from

第七节　字母 R-S

你将在录音中听到五个单词或词组，请将听到的单词或词组与下面题目中含义一致的单词或词组连线。

Exercise 1

题号	单词 / 词组
1	A. prove
2	B. launch
3	C. back to
4	D. enough
5	E. not slow

Exercise 2

题号	单词 / 词组
1	A. twin room
2	B. booking
3	C. books and websites
4	D. senior management positions
5	E. unusual

Exercise 3

题号	单词 / 词组
1	A. improve the situation
2	B. start
3	C. type
4	D. stone carving
5	E. recycled

Exercise 4

题号	单词
1	A. more
2	B. tactics
3	C. leisure
4	D. amazingly
5	E. esteem

Exercise 5

题号	单词 / 词组
1	A. strict
2	B. thin
3	C. learn to
4	D. prevent
5	E. overcome its problems

Exercise 6

题号	单词 / 词组
1	A. dip in the ocean
2	B. miniature
3	C. straightforward
4	D. move to other parts
5	E. sleek

第八节　字母 T-W

你将在录音中听到五个单词或词组，请将听到的单词或词组与下面题目中含义一致的单词或词组连线。

Exercise 1

题号	单词 / 词组
1	A. do activities
2	B. ordinary people
3	C. leading musicians
4	D. wildlife
5	E unreliable

Exercise 2

题号	单词 / 词组
1	A. patterns
2	B. danger
3	C. last
4	D. see the need of
5	E. perform for the first time

Exercise 3

题号	单词/词组
1	A. prominent
2	B. below
3	C. come first in the championship
4	D. the introduction of agriculture
5	E. special

Exercise 4

题号	单词/词组
1	A. tutor
2	B. try out his idea
3	C. stealing
4	D. cultivate
5	E. removing

Exercise 5

题号	单词
1	A. solutions
2	B. double
3	C. rivers
4	D. maximum
5	E. uncooperative

Exercise 6

题号	单词/词组
1	A. transform into
2	B. high
3	C. put up with
4	D. good planning
5	E. rinse off

答案
ANSWERS

Chapter 01　雅思听力真题考点词

第一节　基础考点

一　纯数字

Exercise 1

1. 80	2. 318	3. 9,920	4. 14
5. 385,900	6. 818	7. 1,490	8. 619
9. 78,000	10. 2,800		

Exercise 2

1. 2,280	2. 390	3. 100,000	4. 55,000
5. 889	6. 236,400,000	7. 1,000,000	8. 5,580
9. 4,518	10. 66		

Exercise 3

1. 661,922	2. 1,115	3. 22,100	4. 1,000
5. 980	6. 1,700	7. 131,000	8. 6,600
9. 8,412	10. 10,000		

Exercise 4

1. 50	2. 260,819	3. 581	4. 26
5. 12,520	6. 558	7. 918	8. 19
9. 100	10. 3,182		

二　长数字

Exercise 1

1. 98010231	2. 726940504	3. 23192813121	4. 8920047592
5. 893007792	6. 3281919	7. 310987111	8. 12978083
9. 233888672	10. 264796623		

Exercise 2

1. 800045873	2. 987023221	3. 7826300421	4. 1229870061

5. 2225556729   6. 6644882910   7. 501666832   8. 7832223987

9. 90082741   10. 405067930

Exercise 3

1. 4574592831   2. 7783320001   3. 891007216   4. 765009288

5. 9872361   6. 8002831220   7. 94419829   8. 617289038

9. 287644   10. 568219003

三 字母与数字

Exercise 1

1. G58 1SB   2. LYNE288HG   3. POPA278   4. CV35 0DB

5. DUW05444   6. KIKO230   7. AB14 526   8. FORE5ST

9. 457ELPS   10. RETS628

Exercise 2

1. G88 SH2   2. LOP342MHU   3. FEN1287   4. YIHON8764

5. DPS473   6. THER808   7. 338PAPA   8. GHMM420

9. JHD11 L90   10. CF99 1NA

Exercise 3

1. GRO2180   2. E14 5HQ   3. ARBU808   4. DJ745PQ

5. SCF008   6. ROLS915   7. DH55 4SW   8. COUR541

9. LMNP098   10. SO14 1OB

四 单位

Exercise 1

1. 80 square metres   2. 200 gallons   3. 250 tons   4. 10 centimetres

5. 1,000 amperes   6. 120 hectares   7. 500 miles   8. 3–4 pints

9. $14.80   10. 880 ounces

Exercise 2

1. 80 grams   2. 20 degrees Celsius   3. £7.45   4. 1.4 litres

5. 500,200 kilometres   6. £60.50   7. 280 yards   8. 1,300 cubic metres

9. 6 inches   10. 90 degrees Fahrenheit

五 地址

Exercise 1

1. Station Square   2. Woodside Street   3. 127 Dulwich Road   4. 58 Carter Lane

5. 317 Finchley Road   6. 11 King Street   7. 69 Camden Road   8. 23 Riverside Street

9. Portobello Avenue   10. 14 Bank Road

Exercise 2

1. 20 Great Sutton Street   2. Battersea Road   3. Oxford Street   4. 25 Canonbury Lane

5. No.8 Chelsea Road   6. Anton Street   7. Fernlea Square   8. Crawley Street

9. No.1 Canary Street   10. 15 Islington Road

Exercise 3

1. 13 Ocean Road   2. 5th Avenue   3. Abbey Road   4. 25 Bridge Road

5. 7th Sunflower Avenue   6. Mayfair Avenue   7. 11 Arbuthnot Road   8. Balham Street

9. 46 Smithfield Street   10. No.4 Fleet Lane

六 日期

Exercise 1

1. 27 September   2. 22 June, 1980   3. 24 February, 2000   4. 19 January, 1994

5. 10 August, 1830   6. 15 March   7. May 7, 1919   8. January 1, 2001

9. 11 November   10. 23 March, 2004

Exercise 2

1. 31 January, 1976   2. July 15   3. 8 October, 1949   4. 30 October

5. 22 October   6. July 27   7. 24 December, 1960   8. 21 December

9. March 18, 2018   10. 21 August

Exercise 3

1. 3 February   2. November 12, 2008   3. 29 November, 1988   4. April 19, 1998

5. April 2   6. 23 December, 2005   7. 20 February, 2021   8. September 18, 2015

9. 11 June   10. August 19

七 时间

Exercise 1

1. 6:45   2. 2:20   3. 10:15   4. 10:00

5. 11:05	6. 3:15	7. 10–10.30	8. 5:40
9. 8:46	10. 9:15		

Exercise 2

1. 10:10	2. 7:37	3. 9:25	4. 5:05
5. 10:25	6. 7:16	7. 9:45	8. 8:30
9. 8:50	10. 7:11		

Exercise 3

1. 4:58	2. 7:10	3. 6:18	4. 7:20
5. 8:00	6. 8:58	7. 11:35	8. 9:09
9. 10:55	10. 6:30		

第二节　发音与拼写

多音词

Exercise 1

1. impact v. 对…产生影响	2. contrast n. 差别；差异	3. excuse v. 原谅
4. wind v. 缠绕	5. conduct v. 组织；处理	6. present v. 呈现
7. rebel v. 反叛	8. contract n. 合同	9. contest v. 质疑
10. digest v.（使）消化		

Exercise 2

1. insult n. 辱骂	2. extract n. 提取物	3. perfect v. 提高
4. object v. 反对	5. wound n. 伤口	6. estimate v. 估算
7. project n. 项目	8. minute n. 分钟	9. record v. 记录，记载
10. lead v. 领导		

同音异形词

Exercise 1

1. heal heel	2. dye die	3. pray prey	4. brake break
5. flour flower	6. desert dessert	7. peace piece	8. sail sale
9. scent cent	10. coarse course		

Exercise 2

1. night knight	2. role roll	3. tail tale	4. stair stare

5. isle aisle   6. vain vein   7. buy by   8. bough bow

9. story storey   10. fair fare

三 发音相近词

Exercise 1
1. baggage   2. immoral   3. revenge   4. oral

5. suite   6. bold   7. vision   8. hostel

9. hunger   10. retort

Exercise 2
1. extensive   2. assent   3. sweet   4. statue

5. aboard   6. mission   7. canyon   8. quite

9. resource   10. propose

Exercise 3
1. assemble   2. bulletin   3. tap   4. march

5. contend   6. protest   7. intrude   8. reject

9. source   10. inspiration

Exercise 4
1. elapse   2. brown   3. recent   4. personnel

5. campaign   6. amend   7. patent   8. phrase

9. era   10. latitude

Exercise 5
1. flour   2. blossom   3. collar   4. crown

5. illusion   6. ideal   7. stride   8. assume

9. confident   10. badge

Exercise 6
1. reward   2. require   3. assure   4. deduce

5. angle   6. crude   7. adorn   8. contrast

9. perspective   10. later

Exercise 7
1. socks   2. affect   3. principal   4. kitchen

5. chord   6. incident   7. grasp   8. alone

9. slide   10. ripe

Exercise 8

1. cartoon
2. costume
3. proceed
4. vocation
5. widow
6. contest
7. strive
8. clown
9. flash
10. content

Exercise 9

1. quiet
2. luggage
3. policy
4. distort
5. accent
6. status
7. trip
8. taxi
9. sweat
10. immortal

Exercise 10

1. intensive
2. aspiration
3. inject
4. protect
5. potent
6. bandage
7. acquire
8. ensure
9. accident
10. vacation

四 英、美式拼写

Exercise 1

1. publicise publicize
2. humour humor
3. catalogue catalog
4. endeavour endeavor
5. metre meter
6. offence offense
7. pretence pretense
8. memorise memorize
9. authorise authorize
10. rigour rigor

Exercise 2

1. licence license
2. fertilise fertilize
3. cancelled canceled
4. fuelled fueled
5. neutralise neutralize
6. apologise apologize
7. favourite favorite
8. rumour rumor
9. analyse analyze
10. catalyse catalyze

Exercise 3

1. organise organize
2. savour savor
3. theatre theater
4. fibre fiber
5. litre liter
6. labour labor
7. tumour tumor
8. industrialise industrialize
9. neighbour neighbor
10. recognise recognize

Exercise 1

1. X-ray
2. highly-developed industry
3. U-turn
4. brother-in-law
5. hand-made goods
6. self-employed worker
7. cold-blooded animal
8. face-to-face interview
9. well-dressed
10. long-distance telephone

Exercise 2

1. hard-working employee
2. half-asleep
3. old-style machine
4. a 5-year-old boy
5. self-control
6. funny-looking man
7. full-time job
8. low-risk investment
9. peace-loving people
10. self-respect

六 缩写

Exercise 1

1. European Union
2. automatic teller machine
3. Curriculum Vitae
4. nota bene
5. post meridiem
6. information technology
7. Central Processing Unit
8. Asia-Pacific Economic Cooperation
9. chief executive officer
10. United Parcel Service

Exercise 2

1. portable document format
2. ante meridiem
3. World Trade Organization
4. Unidentified Flying Object
5. point of sales
6. Before Christ
7. barbecue
8. intelligence quotient
9. United Nations Educational, Scientific, and Cultural Organization
10. Global Position System

第三节 高频考点词

一 名词

Exercise 1

1. introduction
2. supply
3. recreation
4. snacks
5. photocopy
6. migration
7. appearance
8. agency
9. shells
10. nets

Exercise 2

1. massage
2. maintenance
3. pipes
4. audience
5. outlets
6. angles
7. starvation
8. garage
9. promotion
10. microscope

Exercise 3

1. department
2. labels
3. musicians
4. museum
5. carpet
6. calculator
7. funder
8. district
9. science
10. majority

Exercise 4

1. period
2. penguin
3. correspondence
4. departure
5. member
6. pyramid
7. vegetarian
8. castle
9. resident
10. telecommunication

Exercise 5

1. future
2. improvement
3. furs
4. specialty
5. clients
6. adaptation
7. playground
8. horror
9. calligraphy
10. candle

Exercise 6

1. maximum
2. minimum
3. electricity
4. plates
5. holes
6. socks
7. uniform
8. dinner
9. puzzle
10. grammar

Exercise 7

1. harvest
2. sightseeing
3. application
4. napkin
5. businessman
6. workshop
7. texts
8. drinks
9. brochure
10. branches

Exercise 8

1. battery
2. palace
3. dancing
4. events
5. occupancy
6. tanker
7. budget
8. frogs
9. magnet
10. mirrors

Exercise 9

1. charities
2. entrance
3. author
4. graduation
5. storeroom
6. teamwork
7. hormones
8. surface
9. biscuits
10. filter

Exercise 10

1. director
2. laundry
3. pocket
4. standard
5. building
6. heading
7. ancestor
8. dolphins
9. appeal
10. basins

Exercise 11

1. treasure
2. management
3. crocodile
4. delivery
5. continent
6. consultation
7. postcode
8. property
9. fabric
10. claws

Exercise 12

1. squirrels
2. membership
3. investment
4. cereal
5. architecture
6. machines
7. potatoes
8. weight
9. disability
10. documentary

Exercise 13

1. duration
2. flexibility
3. underneath
4. aboriginals
5. bricks
6. holidays
7. project
8. symbol
9. portion
10. festival

Exercise 14

1. lawyer
2. seaside
3. films
4. camera
5. weapon
6. awards
7. monitor
8. firework
9. flavour
10. explorer

Exercise 15

1. journalist
2. prints
3. talent
4. temperature
5. client
6. tenant
7. literature
8. courses
9. soybean
10. plaster

Exercise 16

1. discussion
2. weeds
3. trumpet
4. crimes
5. specialist
6. fireplace
7. stairway
8. professor
9. sources
10. agriculture

Exercise 17

1. genes
2. criteria
3. passport
4. circumstance
5. installation
6. ingredient
7. companionship
8. comedy
9. potential
10. seminar

Exercise 18

1. cords	2. creature	3. textile	4. trips
5. biologists	6. barbecue	7. laboratories	8. payment
9. option	10. volcano		

Exercise 19

1. settlers	2. concert	3. caravan	4. marriage
5. signal	6. masonry	7. resources	8. mainland
9. council	10. absence		

Exercise 20

1. design	2. evaluation	3. economy	4. suburb
5. subtitle	6. extract	7. waterfall	8. origin
9. swans	10. vetting		

Exercise 21

1. opposition	2. revision	3. preference	4. balcony
5. celebrity	6. advertisement	7. companies	8. ladybugs
9. expectation	10. difficulties		

Exercise 22

1. responsibilities	2. confidence	3. attitude	4. seafood
5. telephone	6. advice	7. principle	8. penalty
9. communication	10. athlete		

Exercise 23

1. foundation	2. downhill	3. construction	4. insect
5. demand	6. visuals	7. canteen	8. stages
9. sunset	10. wedding		

Exercise 24

1. insurance	2. contribution	3. innocence	4. booklet
5. ecologist	6. fluids	7. antennae	8. scenery
9. eclipse	10. technologist		

Exercise 25

1. nutrition	2. vegetable	3. bats	4. towers
5. clinic	6. newspaper	7. postcards	8. fuels
9. headlines	10. doctor		

Exercise 26

1. crops
2. routine
3. theories
4. keyboard
5. accuracy
6. countries
7. experiment
8. rainfall
9. bacteria
10. inconvenience

Exercise 27

1. knowledge
2. request
3. turbine
4. expansion
5. interviewee
6. destruction
7. volunteer
8. machine
9. architect
10. action

Exercise 28

1. merchants
2. helpers
3. kitchen
4. items
5. photographs
6. supervisor
7. method
8. square
9. platinum
10. million

Exercise 29

1. century
2. completion
3. danger
4. laptops
5. drawer
6. report
7. nature
8. tutorial
9. booths
10. movies

Exercise 30

1. horses
2. fridge
3. intrigue
4. mentor
5. resort
6. ritual
7. locals
8. reservation
9. species
10. conservation

Exercise 31

1. lounge
2. astronomy
3. links
4. campsite
5. fees
6. breakfast
7. sculpture
8. refrigerator
9. ceremony
10. reliance

Exercise 32

1. copper
2. cinema
3. certificate
4. character
5. product
6. laboratory
7. headphone
8. detail
9. intermediaries
10. luxury

Exercise 33

1. poverty
2. quality
3. adults
4. customer
5. respondent
6. farmland
7. publishing
8. studio
9. pilots
10. patient

Exercise 34

1. centre
2. boilers
3. presentation
4. description
5. engineer
6. brushes
7. visibility
8. watering
9. twilight
10. simulation

Exercise 35

1. family
2. advantage
3. professionals
4. mushroom
5. stones
6. tickets
7. punctuality
8. livestock
9. essence
10. knives

Exercise 36

1. recordings
2. ability
3. spelling
4. wheelchair
5. arguments
6. impact
7. champion
8. solution
9. errors
10. publicity

Exercise 37

1. diaries
2. arrival
3. discipline
4. extraction
5. dishwasher
6. valley
7. identity
8. tips
9. celebration
10. emotion

Exercise 38

1. calendar
2. patience
3. priority
4. steamships
5. university
6. collection
7. invoice
8. subject
9. attraction
10. carbon

Exercise 39

1. sliver
2. archaeologist
3. photograph
4. experiences
5. mountain
6. interaction
7. tourism
8. assessment
9. corridors
10. hydrogen

Exercise 40

1. vacation
2. scheme
3. bathroom
4. competitors
5. footwear
6. intelligence
7. penknives
8. setting
9. scenario
10. silver

Exercise 41

1. procedure
2. layout
3. surfing
4. region
5. cycling
6. dinosaur
7. drawback
8. frequency
9. stomach
10. subsidiary

Exercise 42

1. congratulations
2. exams
3. hurricane
4. sizes
5. credit
6. kidney
7. cooker
8. spirit
9. reference
10. chandelier

Exercise 43

1. belief
2. tracks
3. standpoint
4. gloves
5. workforce
6. sponge
7. petrol
8. masterpiece
9. obligation
10. originality

Exercise 44

1. context
2. cuisine
3. deadline
4. beginner
5. parking
6. participation
7. broadcast
8. takeover
9. temple
10. destination

Exercise 45

1. display
2. hotel
3. circulation
4. reception
5. cousin
6. consumption
7. dissatisfaction
8. comment
9. outcome
10. badges

Exercise 46

1. monsters
2. reputation
3. daughter
4. villagers
5. bins
6. vibration
7. exercises
8. employee
9. metallurgy
10. permission

Exercise 47

1. sailing
2. object
3. committee
4. regulation
5. structure
6. entertainment
7. minority
8. language
9. efficiency
10. screen

Exercise 48

1. biography
2. poetry
3. caves
4. climate
5. sanctuary
6. crossbar
7. registration
8. photos
9. string
10. software

Exercise 49

1. nationalities
2. authorization
3. minerals
4. barcode
5. institutions
6. houses
7. requirement
8. signposts
9. glasses
10. sprinter

Exercise 50

1. accounts	2. receiver	3. situation	4. repairs
5. rehearsal	6. clips	7. realism	8. accommodation
9. seabed	10. information		

Exercise 51

1. warehouse	2. applicant	3. demonstration	4. phenomenon
5. months	6. umbrella	7. mastery	8. illustration
9. moisture	10. windsurfing		

Exercise 52

1. lecture	2. changes	3. handle	4. landmarks
5. boots	6. participant	7. manager	8. island
9. definition	10. session		

Exercise 53

1. timetable	2. program	3. drought	4. compensation
5. anxiety	6. tunnel	7. timber	8. update
9. discount	10. counterparts		

Exercise 54

1. objectivity	2. classes	3. stairs	4. corners
5. mammals	6. library	7. gardens	8. cutlery
9. cooperation	10. categories		

Exercise 55

1. toys	2. aspect	3. mirror	4. safety
5. rocks	6. extinguishers	7. emperor	8. grouping
9. cabinet	10. theatre		

Exercise 56

1. module	2. evidence	3. medication	4. mixture
5. vacuum	6. seals	7. journey	8. differences
9. wallpaper	10. characteristic		

Exercise 57

1. export	2. conference	3. evaporation	4. stitches
5. guests	6. cushion	7. predator	8. hospital
9. hazard	10. script		

Exercise 58

1. transaction
2. freshman
3. salads
4. incident
5. blanket
6. packaging
7. combination
8. tablecloth
9. energy
10. transaction

Exercise 59

1. cupboard
2. reminder
3. players
4. cities
5. warning
6. exhibition
7. interest
8. glaciers
9. erosion
10. factories

Exercise 60

1. qualification
2. innovation
3. strips
4. robots
5. population
6. soldier
7. income
8. articles
9. journal
10. profits

Exercise 61

1. hostel
2. politician
3. cheese
4. flight
5. performance
6. negotiations
7. fashion
8. partner
9. strategies
10. motivation

Exercise 62

1. airlines
2. passion
3. tools
4. device
5. baseball
6. cowboy
7. undergraduate
8. commodity
9. competition
10. mites

Exercise 63

1. boards
2. emission
3. workload
4. feature
5. coconut
6. notebook
7. cottage
8. textbook
9. identification
10. reconstruction

Exercise 64

1. degree
2. engineering
3. interpretation
4. bottle
5. length
6. contrast
7. bibliography
8. monarch
9. bicycle
10. saliva

Exercise 65

1. fossil
2. antiques
3. arrangement
4. friction
5. oyster
6. protection
7. consumer
8. apology
9. geography
10. galleries

Exercise 66

1. insight	2. instructor	3. bones	4. environment
5. treatment	6. complaints	7. abstract	8. camp
9. opportunity	10. leaflet		

Exercise 67

1. availability	2. portfolio	3. connectives	4. disagreement
5. comparison	6. seaweed	7. manufacturer	8. perfume
9. proficiency	10. librarian		

Exercise 68

1. altitude	2. helmet	3. current	4. tasks
5. stories	6. fertilizer	7. elements	8. noticeboard
9. bulbs	10. administrator		

Exercise 69

1. leadership	2. flamingo	3. humans	4. talks
5. excavations	6. taxes	7. languages	8. heater
9. package	10. pollen		

Exercise 70

1. system	2. airport	3. underground	4. revenue
5. highway	6. teenagers	7. restaurant	8. statue
9. questionnaire	10. instruction		

Exercise 71

1. vehicle	2. lizards	3. huts	4. psychology
5. multimedia	6. fishing	7. weekend	8. collectors
9. allocation	10. fisherman		

Exercise 72

1. planes	2. antiseptic	3. lecturer	4. facilities
5. background	6. salary	7. advertising	8. dialogue
9. bushes	10. tablet		

Exercise 73

1. loyalty	2. impatience	3. skeleton	4. consultant
5. legislation	6. direction	7. triangle	8. starch
9. sunglasses	10. clothes		

Exercise 74

1. observation
2. threat
3. barriers
4. desert
5. turtle
6. chocolate
7. grades
8. infrastructure
9. carving
10. planets

Exercise 75

1. version
2. services
3. habitant
4. wildlife
5. privacy
6. avenue
7. staircases
8. accident
9. habitat
10. automobiles

Exercise 76

1. religion
2. content
3. culture
4. appliance
5. laptop
6. sandwich
7. obstacles
8. issues
9. transition
10. gender

Exercise 77

1. outbreak
2. cooking
3. digestion
4. interruption
5. samples
6. relatives
7. cement
8. silverwares
9. buffet
10. gases

Exercise 78

1. translation
2. schedule
3. souvenir
4. diversity
5. printing
6. morality
7. diving
8. authority
9. function
10. feelings

Exercise 79

1. viewpoint
2. whales
3. restoration
4. location
5. picnic
6. recommendation
7. handout
8. nightlife
9. childcare
10. cafeteria

Exercise 80

1. protein
2. institute
3. pollution
4. hibernation
5. document
6. helicopter
7. diploma
8. absorber
9. insecticide
10. basement

Exercise 81

1. residents
2. files
3. cotton
4. circle
5. tastes
6. journalism
7. restorers
8. internship
9. opinion
10. accountants

Exercise 82

1. components	2. manufacture	3. rivals	4. printer
5. utensil	6. occupation	7. riders	8. interference
9. trails	10. furniture		

Exercise 83

1. expenses	2. powder	3. habits	4. liquid
5. review	6. shortage	7. exploration	8. profit
9. deposit	10. commission		

Exercise 84

1. medicine	2. section	3. sponsorship	4. alternative
5. footprint	6. pottery	7. inhabitant	8. thermostat
9. scholarship	10. chemist		

Exercise 85

1. enquiry	2. coastline	3. frames	4. deficiency
5. website	6. irrigation	7. bookshop	8. vocabulary
9. mechanism	10. babies		

Exercise 86

1. antifreeze	2. varieties	3. arrows	4. reproduction
5. enlargement	6. conclusion	7. statement	8. tanks
9. texture	10. prices		

Exercise 87

1. rainbow	2. license	3. bedroom	4. rats
5. reduction	6. stickers	7. parents	8. technology
9. waiter	10. disturbance		

Exercise 88

1. experience	2. spider	3. microwave	4. cosmetic
5. victim	6. figure	7. motorbikes	8. passenger
9. button	10. storyline		

Exercise 89

1. traffic	2. cheque	3. investigation	4. faculty
5. plots	6. engine	7. equipment	8. aggressions
9. expert	10. breathing		

Exercise 90

1. costume	2. contact	3. achievement	4. leaves
5. blocks	6. balance	7. pepper	8. pressure
9. photography	10. password		

Exercise 91

1. chairman	2. memories	3. seagulls	4. techniques
5. abstraction	6. platform	7. funding	8. subliminal
9. endorsement	10. branch		

Exercise 92

1. children	2. cellulose	3. computer	4. documentation
5. terrace	6. greenhouse	7. offers	8. purposes
9. effect	10. takeaway		

Exercise 93

1. methodology	2. lifestyle	3. stream	4. graphite
5. advance	6. therapy	7. hotels	8. tolerance
9. balloon	10. poster		

Exercise 94

1. company	2. condition	3. administration	4. zones
5. signature	6. painting	7. ropes	8. donation
9. stores	10. meteorology		

Exercise 95

1. newsletter	2. format	3. instrument	4. freedom
5. friendship	6. waterproof	7. scientist	8. pots
9. activities	10. position		

Exercise 96

1. database	2. researcher	3. feedback	4. material
5. allergies	6. ecology	7. rhythm	8. dolls
9. concentration	10. entitlement		

Exercise 97

1. damage	2. rubbish	3. training	4. parties
5. influence	6. dissertation	7. meals	8. decoration
9. wages	10. recession		

Exercise 98

1. wheels
2. causes
3. dentist
4. disease
5. imagination
6. woodland
7. critic
8. aims
9. assurance
10. guidelines

Exercise 99

1. tortoise
2. chicks
3. dweller
4. builder
5. relocation
6. enrollment
7. worksheet
8. methods
9. transport
10. industries

Exercise 100

1. dolphin
2. calculation
3. shower
4. village
5. stadium
6. climbing
7. transcription
8. pirates
9. compressor
10. relationship

二 动词

Exercise 1

1. observe
2. overestimate
3. snail
4. acknowledge
5. absorb
6. carve
7. interview
8. compensate
9. inhabit
10. perform

Exercise 2

1. exchange
2. enlarge
3. enhance
4. convert
5. achieve
6. refer
7. appoint
8. advertise
9. polish
10. concentrate

Exercise 3

1. attract
2. express
3. indicate
4. receive
5. obtain
6. ski
7. raise
8. destroy
9. replace
10. accept

Exercise 4

1. explain
2. measure
3. highlight
4. appear
5. expand
6. exaggerate
7. increase
8. store
9. exist
10. misunderstand

Exercise 5

1. include	2. witness	3. ignore	4. calculate
5. construct	6. cater	7. socialize	8. exclude
9. detect	10. pose		

Exercise 6

1. impose	2. explode	3. decompose	4. deploy
5. occupy	6. swing	7. compare	8. discover
9. activate	10. stick		

Exercise 7

1. release	2. reserve	3. recruit	4. degrade
5. promote	6. resent	7. arrange	8. contain
9. surprise	10. launch		

Exercise 8

1. register	2. commemorate	3. simplify	4. praise
5. attach	6. produce	7. attend	8. sneeze
9. underline	10. rebuild		

Exercise 9

1. classify	2. donate	3. oversee	4. survive
5. cultivate	6. manage	7. derive	8. allow
9. classify	10. restrict		

Exercise 10

1. varnish	2. suggest	3. bargain	4. install
5. preserve	6. overcome	7. investigate	8. assume
9. originate	10. encourage		

Exercise 11

1. reject	2. evaporate	3. minimize	4. acquire
5. decline	6. distinguish	7. sense	8. attack
9. inspire	10. compost		

Exercise 12

1. appreciate	2. capture	3. decrease	4. submit
5. harden	6. react	7. reveal	8. retrain
9. demonstrate	10. represent		

Exercise 13

1. order
2. complete
3. describe
4. specialize
5. identify
6. overlook
7. recycle
8. apply
9. consult
10. miscalculate

Exercise 14

1. resemble
2. inspect
3. bounce
4. assist
5. range
6. dismiss
7. improve
8. predict
9. ensure
10. contribute

Exercise 15

1. organize
2. grant
3. require
4. provide
5. compete
6. trace
7. migrate
8. adjust
9. purchase
10. conduct

三 形容词

Exercise 1

1. famous
2. drunk
3. overweight
4. dangerous
5. repetitive
6. various
7. theoretical
8. historical
9. minimal
10. dusky

Exercise 2

1. popular
2. portable
3. plastic
4. personal
5. difficult
6. similar
7. unusual
8. transportable
9. seasonal
10. certain

Exercise 3

1. sensitive
2. rare
3. formative
4. captive
5. chemical
6. intense
7. visual
8. stressful
9. retail
10. accurate

Exercise 4

1. smooth
2. intermediate
3. opposite
4. central
5. fatal
6. essential
7. sustainable
8. correct
9. rhetorical
10. entire

Exercise 5

1. formal	2. different	3. moral	4. fragile
5. nocturnal	6. inconvenient	7. precious	8. significant
9. trim	10. total		

Exercise 6

1. influential	2. available	3. reusable	4. reflective
5. unique	6. global	7. convenient	8. integral
9. dramatic	10. optional		

Exercise 7

1. quiet	2. solid	3. impressive	4. mechanical
5. conditional	6. critical	7. anonymous	8. confident
9. electronic	10. uncomfortable		

Exercise 8

1. daily	2. rechargeable	3. deterrent	4. average
5. expensive	6. precise	7. artificial	8. accountable
9. flexible	10. sweet		

Exercise 9

1. bilingual	2. choppy	3. fake	4. parasitic
5. cooperative	6. insufficient	7. grown	8. obedient
9. irrelevant	10. regional		

Exercise 10

1. extra	2. agricultural	3. positive	4. doubtful
5. geographical	6. polytechnic	7. preventable	8. homesick
9. superficial	10. thorough		

Exercise 11

1. peaceful	2. special	3. acceptable	4. comprehensive
5. psychological	6. industrial	7. costal	8. uneven
9. lucky	10. realistic		

Exercise 12

1. biographical	2. professional	3. familiar	4. successful
5. durable	6. massive	7. cruel	8. fluid
9. nutritional	10. negative		

Exercise 13

1. bony	2. inland	3. measurable	4. fantastic
5. edible	6. blind	7. main	8. simple
9. internal	10. workable		

Exercise 14

1. nervous	2. administrative	3. random	4. unclear
5. external	6. disabled	7. cardinal	8. golden
9. commercial	10. gradual		

Exercise 15

1. emotional	2. sugary	3. legal	4. inside
5. cheerful	6. linguistic	7. slippery	8. memorable
9. uneasy	10. immediate		

Exercise 16

1. urban	2. further	3. distinctive	4. worn
5. affordable	6. excessive	7. tight	8. outside
9. prevalent	10. initial		

Exercise 17

1. international	2. regular	3. introductory	4. modern
5. unimportant	6. childish	7. separate	8. dull
9. crystal	10. previous		

Exercise 18

1. moderate	2. ambitious	3. exact	4. faraway
5. tropical	6. complex	7. inadequate	8. unpleasant
9. tailless	10. sour		

Exercise 19

1. renewable	2. coastal	3. organic	4. sociable
5. fresh	6. suitable	7. digestive	8. impractical
9. profitable	10. inaccurate		

Exercise 20

1. genetic	2. multiple	3. obvious	4. valuable
5. comfortable	6. dietary	7. leisure	8. wealthy
9. salty	10. annual		

Exercise 21

1. environmental 　 2. allergic 　 3. attractive 　 4. overall

5. hidden 　 6. radical 　 7. astronomical 　 8. dark

9. underwater 　 10. stable

Exercise 22

1. reliable 　 2. useless 　 3. constant 　 4. interactive

5. overseas 　 6. additional 　 7. electrical 　 8. minor

9. lonely 　 10. current

Exercise 23

1. inefficient 　 2. necessary 　 3. operational 　 4. important

5. unpredictable 　 6. democratic 　 7. effective 　 8. strict

9. smart 　 10. navigational

Exercise 24

1. unhealthy 　 2. compulsory 　 3. automatic 　 4. traditional

5. robotic 　 6. ancient 　 7. poisonous 　 8. executive

9. private 　 10. natural

Exercise 25

1. extinct 　 2. efficient 　 3. nearby 　 4. valid

5. normal 　 6. remote 　 7. unsystematic 　 8. technical

9. archaeological 　 10. stormy

四　副词

Exercise 1

1. originally 　 2. directly 　 3. positively 　 4. quite

5. recently 　 6. virtually 　 7. surprisingly 　 8. spiritually

9. fully 　 10. economically

Exercise 2

1. honestly 　 2. afterwards 　 3. ahead 　 4. initially

5. punctually 　 6. slowly 　 7. quickly 　 8. together

9. especially 　 10. never

Exercise 3

1. fairly
2. normally
3. mainly
4. effectively
5. annually
6. immediately
7. thoroughly
8. globally
9. previously
10. efficiently

Exercise 4

1. easily
2. physically
3. entirely
4. electronically
5. always
6. widely
7. briefly
8. particularly
9. occasionally
10. regularly

五 常考搭配

Exercise 1

1. account for
2. carry out
3. book date
4. be satisfied with
5. work together
6. be able to
7. be close to
8. set up
9. lack of
10. focus on

Exercise 2

1. be covered with
2. at the top of
3. have nothing to do with
4. feed on
5. out of date
6. consist of
7. a feeling of
8. set out
9. be made into
10. show off

Exercise 3

1. the rest of
2. drop off
3. lead to
4. except for
5. keep fit
6. be opposite to
7. be related to
8. learn about
9. look after
10. ask for

Exercise 4

1. link to
2. contribute to
3. extract from
4. dry up
5. pick up
6. sign up
7. be known as
8. depend on
9. switch off
10. think about

Exercise 5

1. convert into
2. be attached to
3. eat out
4. prevent from
5. result in
6. rather than
7. be proud of
8. peak season
9. in detail
10. be caused by

Exercise 6

1. heat up
2. sort out
3. pay attention to
4. high season
5. problem solving
6. be suitable for
7. in the form of
8. at present
9. go aboard
10. raise money

Exercise 7

1. change into
2. rely on
3. bring on
4. out of control
5. in advance
6. tend to
7. be made of
8. look for
9. high altitude
10. wake up

Exercise 8

1. turn to
2. wait for
3. all kinds of
4. at once
5. derive from
6. go around
7. in the future
8. take over
9. compared to
10. benefit from

六 地名及相关词汇

Exercise 1

1. Suez Canal
2. Africa
3. North America
4. Russia
5. India
6. South Pole
7. Alaska
8. the Arctic Ocean
9. Sahara
10. Tower of London

Exercise 2

1. Italy
2. Chicago
3. Panama Canal
4. the Mediterranean
5. Sydney Opera House
6. Venice
7. Washington D.C.
8. South America
9. China
10. Europe

Exercise 3

1. Central Park
2. North Pole
3. Sydney
4. New Zealand
5. Moscow
6. Australia
7. Latin America
8. New York City
9. Indonesia
10. Mount Fuji

Exercise 4

1. Greece
2. Eiffel Tower
3. the Pacific Ocean
4. Asia
5. Hollywood
6. Pyramids
7. Taj Mahal
8. Wellington
9. Victoria Falls
10. England

Exercise 5

1. Rome
2. America
3. Switzerland
4. Canada
5. Oxford
6. Statue of Liberty
7. Westminster Abbey
8. Disneyland
9. Great Barrier Reef
10. Scotland

Chapter 02 雅思听力场景词汇

第一节 住宿（Accommodation）

Exercise 1

1. balcony
2. elevator
3. northern
4. fire gate
5. house agency
6. water bill
7. insurance
8. shower
9. attic
10. privacy

Exercise 2

1. toilet
2. single room
3. dining room
4. living room
5. cloakroom
6. hotel
7. city centre
8. heater
9. corridor
10. suburbs

Exercise 3

1. corner
2. car park
3. road
4. garden
5. swimming pool
6. rental price
7. no smoking
8. neighbour
9. towel
10. cabinet

Exercise 4

1. gas bill
2. deposit
3. facilities
4. split
5. minimum rent
6. pillow
7. curtain
8. youth hostel
9. guest house
10. sofa

Exercise 5

1. roommate
2. street
3. water heater
4. homestay
5. microwave oven
6. dishwasher
7. countryside
8. lounge
9. refundable
10. ladder

Exercise 6

1. southern
2. garage
3. leak
4. layout
5. rural area
6. urban area
7. south
8. radiator
9. contact
10. washing machine

Exercise 7

1. toaster	2. twin room	3. cushion	4. utility bill
5. shared kitchen	6. carpet	7. refrigerator	8. water closet
9. pet	10. property owner		

Exercise 8

1. vacuum cleaner	2. lamp	3. guest	4. courtyard
5. avenue	6. cooker	7. dormitory	8. private property
9. cabin	10. landlord		

Exercise 9

1. electricity bill	2. standard suite	3. furniture	4. maximum rent
5. tenant	6. eastern	7. environment	8. apartment
9. lane	10. laundry room		

Exercise 10

1. contract	2. fountain	3. air conditioner	4. host family
5. stove	6. phone bill	7. contract	8. fountain
9. blanket	10. house agent		

第二节 饮食（Food and Drink）

Exercise 1

1. butter	2. restaurant	3. dessert	4. food allergies
5. buffet	6. corn	7. red pepper	8. crab
9. spicy	10. yogurt		

Exercise 2

1. chocolate bar	2. balanced diet	3. lobster	4. cocktail
5. cucumber	6. lamb	7. special diet	8. red meat
9. cabbage	10. bread		

Exercise 3

1. beverage	2. oyster	3. café	4. fish and chips
5. bitter	6. take-away	7. main course	8. biscuit
9. mushroom	10. cheese		

Exercise 4

1. sauce
2. pizza
3. salad bar
4. meat
5. napkin
6. steak
7. plate
8. hotdog
9. bean
10. wine

Exercise 5

1. pork
2. salty
3. menu
4. soup
5. bowl
6. chicken
7. bakery
8. beef
9. honey
10. bacon

Exercise 6

1. vegetarian
2. cuisine
3. snack bar
4. pudding
5. shrimp
6. hamburger
7. spoon
8. fork
9. mineral water
10. fruit juice

Exercise 7

1. curry
2. pub
3. sugar
4. snacks
5. junk food
6. sour
7. flour
8. dining hall
9. carrot
10. vegetable

Exercise 8

1. delicious
2. noodle
3. nut
4. strawberry
5. dairy product
6. cafeteria
7. alcohol
8. seafood
9. onion
10. pumpkin

第三节　旅游（Travel）

Exercise 1

1. tourism
2. campsite
3. souvenir
4. safety helmet
5. sandals
6. Chicago
7. aquarium
8. tour guide
9. cancel
10. thunderstorm

Exercise 2

1. steam engine ship
2. first aid kit
3. bottled water
4. minibus
5. sharp corner
6. cousin
7. railway station
8. Great Barrier Reef
9. special offer
10. in advance

Exercise 3

1. refund
2. embassy
3. delay
4. horse riding
5. booklet
6. hiking
7. Tower of London
8. cycling route
9. gift shop
10. rescue

Exercise 4

1. Sydney
2. organic farm
3. coastal area
4. Toronto
5. Sydney Opera House
6. rubber shoes
7. video camera
8. telescope
9. Northern Ireland
10. wire

Exercise 5

1. comfortable clothes
2. New Zealand
3. book a ticket
4. accident
5. walking boots
6. travel agency
7. ferry
8. Scotland
9. Washington D.C.
10. main entrance

Exercise 6

1. nationality
2. rain boots
3. tent
4. gloves
5. self-drive tour
6. tourist brochure
7. mosquito net
8. mileage
9. driving license
10. transfer

Exercise 7

1. camping
2. schedule
3. round-trip ticket
4. emergency contact person
5. fishing
6. payment
7. rope
8. backpacker
9. cookery lesson
10. transportation

Exercise 8

1. radio
2. life jacket
3. adventure
4. single ticket
5. cruise
6. information centre
7. risk
8. digital camera
9. smartphone
10. one-way ticket

Exercise 9

1. safety regulation
2. passport
3. noticeboard
4. personal belongings
5. weather observation
6. charity event
7. extra charge
8. internet access
9. tropical diseases
10. thief

Exercise 10

1. package tour
2. motorcycle
3. sight-seeing
4. alarm system
5. coach
6. stamp
7. identification card
8. traffic
9. rock climbing
10. credit card

Exercise 11

1. torch
2. vehicle
3. balloon ride
4. telegraph
5. sleeping bag
6. Canada
7. Australia
8. bus stop
9. New York
10. confirm

Exercise 12

1. massage
2. compass
3. helicopter trip
4. sunglasses
5. shopping
6. raincoat
7. bush walk
8. surfing
9. sunscreen
10. survival course

Exercise 13

1. lip balm
2. express train
3. picnic
4. canoe
5. destination
6. drifting
7. make a reservation
8. theme park
9. plane
10. shuttle bus

Exercise 14

1. double-decker bus
2. caravan
3. harbour
4. lorry
5. bay
6. tram
7. offspring
8. cable car
9. return ticket
10. timetable

Exercise 15

1. airport
2. duty-free shop
3. direct flight
4. first class
5. business class
6. economy class
7. departure
8. arrival
9. vacant seat
10. check in

Exercise 16

1. rush hour
2. wheel
3. engine
4. brake
5. wheelchair
6. platform
7. pick-up point
8. hitch-hike
9. spot
10. accommodation package

Exercise 17

1. country
2. cottage
3. village
4. town
5. lookout point
6. scenery
7. landmark
8. historical interest
9. waterfall
10. museum

Exercise 18

1. cinema
2. church
3. art gallery
4. pyramid
5. safari park
6. mountain
7. desert
8. tunnel
9. hot spring
10. canal

Exercise 19

1. beach	2. cave	3. castle	4. palace
5. ancient temple	6. island	7. bridge	8. tropical rainforest
9. wetland	10. marsh		

Exercise 20

1. amusement park	2. playground	3. pottery factory	4. workshop
5. teenager	6. agriculture fair	7. city hall	8. craft shop
9. conference center	10. post office		

第四节　健康（Health）

Exercise 1

1. nutrition	2. wrist	3. capsule	4. palm
5. allergy	6. toothache	7. vaccinate	8. dizzy
9. knee	10. kidney		

Exercise 2

1. X-ray	2. herb	3. bad eyesight	4. injection
5. surgery	6. toe	7. blood pressure	8. epidemic
9. medicine	10. antibiotics		

Exercise 3

1. mental	2. health center	3. nails	4. precaution
5. fever	6. forehead	7. hospital	8. ambulance
9. medical center	10. scar		

Exercise 4

1. tropical disease	2. brain	3. jaw	4. mouth
5. sore throat	6. yellow fever	7. shoulder	8. tablet
9. waist	10. wound		

Exercise 5

1. side effects	2. eye drops	3. back trouble	4. diagnose
5. prescribe	6. virus	7. bone	8. memory
9. ankle	10. make an appointment		

Exercise 6

1. dentist
2. therapy
3. surgeon
4. vitamin
5. patient
6. headache
7. physical therapy
8. physician
9. finger
10. poisonous

Exercise 7

1. lung
2. disturbing
3. pulse
4. painkiller
5. elbow
6. bacteria
7. nurse
8. symptom
9. flu
10. vet

Exercise 8

1. catch a cold
2. pill
3. treatment
4. heart rate
5. stiff neck
6. stuffed nose
7. protein
8. cough
9. chest infection
10. cell

第五节 社会生活（Social Life）

Exercise 1

1. budget
2. chess
3. receipt
4. band
5. jogging
6. baseball
7. coach
8. carnival
9. cotton
10. volleyball

Exercise 2

1. single item
2. checklist
3. fancy dress
4. shopping online
5. textile
6. convenience store
7. comedy
8. promotion
9. cellist
10. stretch

Exercise 3

1. table tennis
2. guitar
3. tennis
4. audience
5. silver cloth
6. squash
7. curved
8. annual fee
9. weight training
10. invoice

Exercise 4

1. violin
2. formal clothes
3. suit
4. trumpet
5. drum
6. football
7. decoration balloons
8. fashionable
9. dark trousers
10. string instrument

Exercise 5

1. jazz music	2. subtitle	3. department store	4. poster
5. display	6. reasonable price	7. grocery store	8. uniform
9. shop assistant	10. pianist		

Exercise 6

1. tragedy	2. roller-skating	3. pattern	4. best buy
5. science fiction movie	6. sportswear	7. traditional	8. supply
9. music festival	10. kick-boxing		

Exercise 7

1. relaxation	2. piano	3. subscription	4. rehearse
5. exhibition	6. sound effect	7. skiing	8. bowling
9. skirt	10. perfume		

Exercise 8

1. relaxation	2. piano	3. subscription	4. rehearse
5. exhibition	6. sound effect	7. skiing	8. bowling
9. skirt	10. perfume		

Exercise 9

1. documentary	2. cartoon	3. jeans	4. cello
5. spare socks	6. concert hall	7. dance studio	8. keyboard
9. snow-boarding	10. membership		

Exercise 10

1. costume	2. hobby	3. sweater	4. microphone
5. badminton	6. yoga	7. retail chain	8. satisfactory
9. casual clothes	10. shopping mall		

第六节　工作（Work）

Exercise 1

1. commuter	2. staff	3. interviewee	4. craftsmen
5. leadership	6. job applicant	7. confidence	8. designer
9. vacancy	10. annual interest rate		

Exercise 2

1. mortgage	2. colleague	3. password	4. recruit
5. flexible working time	6. programmer	7. bank statement	8. carpenter
9. merchant bank	10. signature		

Exercise 3

1. accountant	2. hairdresser	3. interviewer	4. service charge
5. occupation	6. valid	7. qualification	8. debt
9. medical insurance	10. low-interest loan		

Exercise 4

1. penny	2. insurance policy	3. application form	4. experienced
5. clear voice	6. permanent staff	7. overdraw	8. emotion
9. domestic bank	10. waiter		

Exercise 5

1. journalist	2. frequency	3. respect	4. job arrangements
5. exchange rate	6. paid vacation	7. night shift	8. coffee break
9. security	10. project manager		

Exercise 6

1. employee	2. engineer	3. opportunity for promotion	
4. director	5. communication skills	6. certificate	7. employment
8. withdraw	9. overseas bank	10. employer	

Exercise 7

1. job duties	2. job interview	3. attitude	4. social ability
5. academic background	6. deposit account	7. personality	8. day shift
9. full-time job	10. receptionist		

Exercise 8

1. tidy	2. temporary staff	3. coin	4. value
5. job responsibility	6. open an account	7. self-employed	8. commercial bank
9. police officer	10. cleaner		

第七节 教育（Education）

Exercise 1

1. literature 2. seminar 3. Bachelor's degree 4. extension
5. inaccurate 6. computer science 7. linguistics 8. training session
9. necessary 10. finance

Exercise 2

1. deadline 2. arts 3. primary school 4. workshop
5. semester 6. submit 7. supervisor 8. enrollment fee
9. engineering 10. projector

Exercise 3

1. attention 2. absence 3. journalism 4. note-taking skill
5. reasonable excuse 6. efficiency 7. silent 8. science
9. statistics 10. proposal

Exercise 4

1. architecture 2. psychology 3. fine arts 4. anthropology
5. paper 6. social network 7. collect data 8. sophomore
9. registration 10. evaluation

Exercise 5

1. physics 2. astronomy 3. questionnaire 4. dropout
5. coordinator 6. mass media 7. professor 8. support
9. junior 10. counselor

Exercise 6

1. intensive course 2. transcript 3. teaching assistant 4. biology
5. subject 6. intermediate course 7. lecturer 8. credit
9. technique 10. candidate

Exercise 7

1. regular exercise 2. group discussion 3. reliable source 4. essay
5. assessment methods 6. postgraduate 7. case study 8. tutor
9. physical education 10. grade

Exercise 8

1. problem-solving 2. modular course 3. presentation 4. geography

5. priority   6. record   7. observation   8. field trip

9. periodical   10. senior

Exercise 9

1. database   2. confusion   3. faculty/office staff   4. failure

5. optional course   6. scanner   7. compulsory course   8. disruption

9. catalogue   10. beginning course

Exercise 10

1. handout   2. attendance rate   3. written work   4. ceremony

5. undergraduate   6. lecture   7. excellent   8. chemistry

9. experiment   10. associate professor

Exercise 11

1. achievement   2. time management   3. speech   4. minor

5. student advisor   6. advanced course   7. representative   8. tutorial

9. major   10. recall

Exercise 12

1. bullying   2. assignment   3. financial problems   4. feedback

5. study diary   6. freshman   7. secretary   8. dean

9. task   10. detail

Exercise 13

1. secondary school   2. basic course   3. orientation week   4. due-date

5. diploma   6. tape recorder   7. economics   8. certificate

9. theoretical framework   10. thesis

Exercise 14

1. dissertation   2. bibliography   3. project   4. subject

5. reference   6. final draft   7. outline   8. structure

9. abstract   10. summary

Exercise 15

1. assumption   2. objective   3. research   4. investigation

5. cover page   6. contents page   7. literature review   8. subheading

9. circulation desk   10. paragraph

第八节 讲座（Lecture）

Exercise 1

1. evaporate	2. cloudy	3. production	4. flood
5. waste disposal	6. traffic density	7. ocean currents	8. consumption
9. fossil fuels	10. recycling material		

Exercise 2

1. slave	2. destruction	3. garbage	4. slang
5. monitor	6. culture	7. import	8. crystal
9. weather	10. competition		

Exercise 3

1. constant supply	2. carbon dioxide	3. hunting	4. takeover
5. acid rain	6. rainy	7. comet	8. planet
9. sustainable development		10. renewable resources	

Exercise 4

1. alternative energy	2. investment	3. cultivate	4. solid
5. market share	6. influence	7. snowy	8. atmosphere
9. corporate crime	10. cooperation		

Exercise 5

1. irrigation	2. predictable	3. natural resources	4. clay
5. oxygen	6. water treatment	7. export	8. public awareness
9. insect	10. deforestation		

Exercise 6

1. vision	2. global warming	3. petrol	
4. international cooperation		5. geographical features	
6. warehouse	7. profit	8. habitat	9. stock market
10. iron			

Exercise 7

1. population	2. ecosystem	3. ozone layer	4. emission
5. greenhouse effect	6. mediator	7. wind force	8. industry
9. tide	10. language		

Exercise 8

1. shady	2. firewood	3. electric power plants	4. temperature
5. nuclear power plants	6. expansion	7. superiority	8. drought
9. distortion	10. fog		

Exercise 9

1. parasite	2. solar energy	3. dweller	4. advertising
5. raw material	6. skeleton	7. cliff	8. manufacture
9. factory	10. erosion		

Exercise 10

1. innovation	2. logo	3. race	4. metal
5. windy	6. campaign	7. coal	8. liquid
9. creative	10. humid		

Exercise 11

1. plastic collection	2. conservation	3. dolphin	4. democratic
5. weed	6. mine	7. plain	8. filter
9. update	10. capital		

Exercise 12

1. container	2. oil	3. solution	4. sales figure
5. mineral	6. climate change	7. air quality	8. rainfall
9. technology	10. timber		

Exercise 13

1. marketing strategy	2. lifestyle	3. strike	4. cost control
5. wood	6. tax	7. bamboo	8. marble
9. satellite	10. wildlife		

Exercise 14

1. rare breeds animal	2. creature	3. gene pool	4. kangaroo
5. ancestor	6. dinosaur	7. endangered species	8. extinct species
9. fox	10. reptile		

Exercise 15

1. snake	2. diversity	3. crocodile	4. mammal
5. zebra	6. elephant	7. lion	8. wolf
9. threaten	10. deer		

Chapter 03　听力同义替换词表

第一节　字母 A–B

Exercise 1

1-D　2-C　3-A　4-E　5-B

Exercise 2

1-A　2-E　3-B　4-C　5-D

Exercise 3

1-C　2-A　3-B　4-E　5-D

Exercise 4

1-D　2-B　3-A　4-C　5-E

Exercise 5

1-B　2-E　3-D　4-C　5-A

Exercise 6

1-C　2-A　3-E　4-B　5-D

第二节　字母 C

Exercise 1

1-E　2-A　3-B　4-C　5-D

Exercise 2

1-C　2-D　3-B　4-E　5-A

Exercise 3

1-D　2-A　3-B　4-E　5-C

Exercise 4

1-B　2-E　3-C　4-A　5-D

Exercise 5

1-A　2-C　3-E　4-B　5-D

Exercise 6

1-D　2-A　3-E　4-C　5-B

第三节　字母 D–F

Exercise 1

1-C　2-E　3-A　4-B　5-D

Exercise 2

1-E　2-C　3-B　4-A　5-D

Exercise 3

1-D　2-B　3-E　4-C　5-A

Exercise 4

1-E　2-D　3-C　4-A　5-B

Exercise 5

1-B　2-A　3-D　4-E　5-C

Exercise 6

1-E　2-D　3-C　4-B　5-A

第四节 字母 G–I

Exercise 1

1-C 2-D 3-E 4-A 5-B

Exercise 2

1-A 2-D 3-E 4-C 5-B

Exercise 3

1-B 2-E 3-C 4-D 5-A

Exercise 4

1-B 2-A 3-D 4-E 5-C

Exercise 5

1-E 2-B 3-A 4-C 5-D

Exercise 6

1-C 2-A 3-D 4-E 5-B

第五节 字母 J–N

Exercise 1

1-E 2-C 3-B 4-A 5-D

Exercise 2

1-C 2-E 3-A 4-B 5-D

Exercise 3

1-C 2-A 3-B 4-D 5-E

Exercise 4

1-C 2-A 3-B 4-E 5-D

Exercise 5

1-B 2-C 3-E 4-D 5-A

Exercise 6

1-B 2-D 3-A 4-E 5-C

第六节 字母 O–Q

Exercise 1

1-A 2-E 3-D 4-B 5-C

Exercise 2

1-B 2-A 3-E 4-D 5-C

Exercise 3

1-E 2-A 3-D 4-C 5-B

Exercise 4

1-C 2-E 3-D 4-A 5-B

Exercise 5

1-E 2-D 3-A 4-B 5-C

Exercise 6

1-D 2-A 3-B 4-E 5-C

第七节 字母 R–S

Exercise 2

1-D 2-A 3-E 4-C 5-B

Exercise 1

1-C 2-B 3-A 4-E 5-D

Exercise 3

1-B 2-A 3-D 4-E 5-C

Exercise 4

1-C 2-D 3-A 4-B 5-E

Exercise 5

1-E 2-A 3-D 4-B 5-C

Exercise 6

1-D 2-C 3-B 4-E 5-A

第八节　字母 T–W

Exercise 1

1-B 2-C 3-D 4-E 5-A

Exercise 2

1-D 2-A 3-B 4-C 5-E

Exercise 3

1-B 2-D 3-C 4-E 5-A

Exercise 4

1-E 2-A 3-D 4-B 5-C

Exercise 5

1-C 2-D 3-E 4-B 5-A

Exercise 6

1-C 2-E 3-A 4-B 5-D